Feast into Mourning

On a blazing hot Sunday afternoon the parishioners of St Oswald's church are out in force to support relatives and friends in the annual parish cricket match. The weekend has been a hectic one, for St Oswald's is celebrating its patronal festival, and the spectators are happy to relax in the August heat. Only sixteen-year-old Zoe Morgan is bored. So she decides to walk up to a nearby spinney to search for an earring she lost there the night before. But someone else has been in the spinney; someone who has committed a terrible crime . . .

Zoe's discovery of the body heralds the start of an extraordinary murder investigation for Chief Inspector Browne and Detective Sergeant Hunter. For the charred and decaying corpse yields no ready clues and vital time is lost before the identity of the victim can finally be confirmed. The pressure mounts as Inspector Browne, Sergeant Hunter and their colleagues delve into church politics and the victim's family history in order to uncover a motive for the savage murder. But their enquiries are conducted amongst a local community which is swiftly closing ranks . . . A community which, Browne is convinced, harbours a killer in its midst.

Feast into Mourning

Pauline Bell

MACMILLAN
LONDON

First published 1991 by
MACMILLAN LONDON LIMITED
Cavaye Place London SW10 9PG
and Basingstoke

Associated companies in Auckland, Delhi, Dublin, Gaborone,
Hamburg, Harare, Hong Kong, Johannesburg, Kuala Lumpur,
Lagos, Manzini, Melbourne, Mexico City, Nairobi, New York,
Singapore and Tokyo

ISBN 0-333-56773-0

A CIP catalogue record for this book is available from the
British Library

Typeset by Pan Macmillan Limited

Printed and bound in Great Britain by Billing and Sons Limited,
Worcester

Chapter 1

Zoe heaved a deep sigh. She had already wasted half a bright Sunday afternoon on this outdated game, played in ridiculous costumes, the two innings about to be punctuated by children's tea party food. She wriggled round for a pitying stare at the ladies behind her who would shortly depart to the church hall to set it out. Meeting her mother's eye she hastily dropped her gaze so as not to be roped in to help them and began a desultory conversation with the old man in the canvas chair beside her who seemed absorbed in the match.

In spite of her contempt for the cricketers' old-fashioned attire she had aped it with her own white slacks and white vee-necked sweater, topped with a saucy boater. The resulting emphasis on her sexuality was not deliberately sought after. It was merely that she knew by instinct how to create that effect. Her appearance looked 'right' to her when it was nicely provocative. In most other ways, too, her attitudes and opinions were entirely suitable for a girl of sixteen.

She considered her mother, happily swapping recipes behind her, but only in her mind's eye, not risking another turn of the head. She wished she were not so smug with her plump arms and rounded figure and sculptured hair. She surely didn't have to dress in tailored linen with a chaste string of pearls, neat button earrings, pink lipstick and practically no eye make-up. Anyone would think Zoe had taught her nothing. Christine! She even had a smug name. And on this glorious summer day she was knitting an Aran sweater!

Her own sweater was making Zoe uncomfortably hot. With a sinuous wriggle she peeled it off, pulled her shirt tails out of her slacks and tied them under her bust, displaying a bare and nicely browned midriff. The old man, unaware of the envy of the other male spectators, decided to give this buxom and spirited lass the benefit of the finer points of the game. 'Yer'll not see a better text-book cover drive than yon from young Morgan theer,' he offered.

This was lost on Zoe, but she appreciated his goodwill, nodded politely and regarded 'young Morgan' who happened to be her uncle Gerald. Further commentary from old Mr Medway was interspersed with the trite but appreciative comments made on their pleasant surroundings by the band of tea ladies. In a minute, Zoe knew, one of them, in a burst of creative originality, would observe that the walled fields, rising up the hillside opposite them, looked 'just like a patchwork quilt'. She gazed at the oblongs of varying greens and ragged outcrops of heather that rose steeply above the cropped grass and the white-clad players, and decided that the hackneyed comparison was valid provided that the quilt you had in mind had survived several generations of use so that its patches were faded and its seams and bindings frayed.

There was a ripple of applause as Uncle Gerald further distinguished himself, but Zoe, unimpressed, reached under her deck chair for her copy of *Fast Forward*. She opened it to the centre pages and was confronted with a larger-than-life photograph of Shaun Shannon, the lead singer of Jam on It. She regarded the heavy, almost negroid features and sensual mouth, read the print beneath them and tried to decide whether Frank too could be described as 'smouldering'. Certainly he had the same dark hair, heavy features and thick brows and a similar way of ducking his head so that his eyes were overshadowed by them. But Frank's hair curled loosely like his father's and his eyes were blue and almost always smiling and didn't smoulder at all. And his grin showed square white teeth. Not that he'd grinned much in the last few days, at least not at her. She raised her eyes to the improvised cricket pitch and watched him as he walked back to begin his run up, polishing the red ball to the detriment of his clean flannels.

'Just like a patchwork quilt,' announced Annette Hunter, triumphantly, behind her.

Zoe wondered where the narky detective sergeant's wife, with her twee duvet covers and her aspirations to water beds, had become acquainted with patchwork quilts. She waited to see if one of these domestically orientated ladies would notice the similarity between the stone tracery on the church tower and her

8

mother's piece of Aran knitting but the ball Frank had delivered had bounced over her head and had fallen amongst the ladies who scattered to avoid it. The scorer added four to Gerald Morgan's total and the ladies, since they had got to their feet, decided to cross the road to the church hall and begin preparing tea.

'Needs to learn a bit about field placing, that young man o'yourn,' Mr Medway informed Zoe. 'Nice bit of off-spin, ball hit t'shoulder o'the bat, batsman didn't know where the hell it had gone and no bloody fielder to collect.' However, Frank earned a nod of approval from the old man when, two balls later, he removed the middle stump. A polite smattering of applause expressed appreciation of Uncle Gerald's score of twenty-seven and was prolonged to acknowledge the vicar's arrival at the crease in his place. The Reverend Philip Garside judged himself no mean batsman and after considering the matter at his leisure, asked for middle and leg. Mr Medway was not fooled. 'Prattin' about!' he confided to Zoe. 'After all that palaver 'e'll close 'is bloody eyes when t'bloody ball gets anywhere near 'im.' Uncertain how exactly the vicar had offended, Zoe smiled and accepted a peppermint.

Five minutes and two runs later, the vicar justified the old man's poor opinion of him, striding down the wicket to a ball that ripped past him and into the keeper's hand for a stumping. The next man in was a choir member of such seeming antiquity to Zoe that she wondered if he would make it out to the middle. Mr Medway assured her that he was very nifty and could play his shots, which he proceeded to demonstrate, hitting Frank for two fours. The language of Mr Medway's commentary became less sanguinary as the vicar, having removed his pads, began to circulate among the spectators, making the sort of remarks parishioners expect to hear on such occasions as this. He reminded Mr Medway, unnecessarily, Zoe was sure, of the fifty he had knocked on this same festival occasion five years before, then grinned at Zoe. 'Well, Omega, you've picked a good teacher if you want to understand the game. Where's Alpha? I want to enquire after her family.'

Zoe indicated Anne-Marie, sprawled on a rug under a tree a few yards away, scribbling busily in a large diary. Zoe's mother, temporarily in charge of both girls, had suggested that they should sit together in the shade, and, for a while, conscious of the contrast her own vivid face made with Anne-Marie's which was sweating and flushed to an unbecoming strawberry pink, Zoe had complied. A deep tan and contrasting sun-bleached hair, however, need considerable maintenance work and she felt moved to return to the sun.

Besides, it was kinder not to sunbathe next to Anne-Marie. Zoe pitied her for her stick-thin white limbs and little-girl hairstyle. No wonder she'd been chosen for St Oswald's page in the pageant. No one else who was old enough to learn the lines was flat and shapeless and small enough. She couldn't do anything about Anne-Marie's shape but she had tried to take her social education in hand, lending her *Fast Forward* every week as soon as she'd read it. Anne-Marie was still a fan of girl singers though, when she wasn't preoccupied with her crushes on women teachers. There was nothing swervy about her, Zoe decided generously. She was just a case of arrested development. She could remember going through the same stages herself when she was ten or eleven.

Anne-Marie had stopped scribbling and given her attention to the vicar's enquiries for the health of her grandmother in hospital and her mother, unwell at home. 'Frank and I can manage everything,' she assured him, 'especially as Daddy's away just now. We haven't got him to look after.' Daddy! At her age. Zoe cast her eyes up at this lost cause.

The vicar moved on to a group of old ladies and Anne-Marie resumed her diary writing with something approaching animation. Zoe asked herself what, in Anne-Marie's uneventful life, she could have so much to write about. She was probably making it all up, writing what she would like to have happened to her! From time to time she consulted a little pink leaflet before resuming her narrative. Zoe's curiosity was aroused and she decided to stroll casually across to investigate. Anyway, she was sick of being glared at by that snobby policeman's wife who ought to have been helping her mother in the church hall.

Approaching Anne-Marie from behind, she flopped down beside her, startling her, and causing her, as she had hoped, to drop the leaflet. Anne-Marie hurriedly retrieved it but not before Zoe had read the cover. 'Some facts about AIDS.' What on earth did Anne-Marie want with that? Come to think of it she had shown an unexpected interest in that film Miss Atkins had shown them in last week's Social Studies lesson. It had come as a timely warning to Zoe herself and she felt a bit ashamed now of calling Frank a spoilsport. With all his Catholic relations, he probably didn't believe in contraception, though Theresa seemed to have found some way to confine her offspring to just Frank and Anne-Marie.

Zoe rolled over to expose her back to the dappled sunshine under the tree and watched a caterpillar as it fell from a blade of grass on to a stone. It retreated into a crevice and rolled itself into a ball, from which its top end emerged, swaying around in a vain attempt to find the blade it had fallen from. Giving up, it made a bridge by walking its back end towards its front, then moved forward until it was flat again. Zoe felt sorry for it, picked it up and dropped it back into the grass. Returning her attention to the cricket, she was in time to see the verger neatly caught out by a member of the youth club. Her father, following him to the crease, had only two balls to face before the scheduled fifteen overs of the first innings were completed. Zoe began to cheer up. She should have twenty minutes now to talk to Frank before he opened the innings for the under-twenty-fives. Then, if she was lucky and he was out quickly, the rest of the afternoon might be slightly less boring.

Mr Medway was not pleased. 'Supposed to be a church cricket match,' he observed, morosely, 'not an exhibition game for club players who put in an odd appearance at t'youth club an' nivver show their bloody faces on a Sunday.' He glared at the offending youth who had fielded at first slip and picked up the sharp chance the verger had offered.

Frank, leading his team off the field, overheard and paused in front of the old man. 'Couldn't have made up my eleven without him, sir.' Mollified by the civil form of address, Mr Medway began to offer Frank advice on his stroke play. Zoe, who considered Anne-Marie's extreme politeness a symptom of her immaturity, found the same quality appealing in her brother.

She waited for him to join the pair of them but presently realised this was not Frank's intention. He squatted in front of Mr Medway's canvas chair, surrounded by his ten team-mates, and considered adjustments to his batting order. Zoe felt her irritation turn to anger. She had spent this glorious afternoon sitting decorously – well, more or less decorously – in a deck chair whilst her current gentleman friend, in company with twenty-one other white-clad loons, capered on the town moor with a little red ball and six sticks. Now there was a twenty minute break in the proceedings and he wasn't going to speak to her, to appreciate her indulgence and patience. Well, he knew what he could do. There were plenty more fish in the sea and she'd never had any trouble catching them. The problem was that all the immediately available young men were in the group of twelve engrossed in match tactics. If she'd known what she knew now she wouldn't have walked in the spinney with Frank yesterday evening and then she wouldn't have lost her gold dolphin earring.

The heat beat down and in spite of her anger Zoe luxuriated in it with a glorious sense of well-being. The sky was white not blue and, except for the copper beech that grew beside the west door and glowed against the slate roof of the nave, the leaves and branches of the churchyard trees made black silhouettes on it. The houses that faced the moor were a haze of grey-brown millstone grit and baked faded green of gardens. To her right a splash of colour was provided by a wire litter bin, half full of garish wrappers from ices and sweets consumed by the spectators. It would have been considerably fuller if they had taken more trouble with their aim. Zoe frowned with distaste at the motley array of litter that surrounded it.

Moss was encroaching on the old flags that ran along the lower edge of the grass. The flags had absorbed the heat till they could take no more and it shimmered above them. Another day or two of this weather and the moss would dry up and die but this afternoon it was still making a scalloped velvet edging. Zoe turned the other way and regarded the pretentious drinking fountain. No longer functional, it was nonetheless imposing with its stepped pedestal and little marble columns crowned with fancy wrought-iron scrolls. Further across, a sparse crop of Rugby posts held their white arms faithfully aloft waiting for this spurious game to be over and for the season and conditions for a real sport to arrive again.

A determined lady cyclist passed, hauling on her pedals. Zoe wondered what was sufficiently important to cause her to make such an uncomfortable effort. The woman's buttocks overhung her saddle and Zoe felt a mixture of pity and contempt. When she glanced across at the church, the leaves of the topmost branch of a sycamore showed irritating glimpses of the clock face on the tower but the lower branches shaded the porch and kept the sun from blistering the blue and gold paintwork of the notice-board.

Zoe stood up. She'd go and look for her earring now. She probably wouldn't find it but at least when Sir Frank came back to earth and decided to acknowledge her existence, he wouldn't find her waiting around in humiliating fashion for him to notice her.

Anne-Marie asked, lazily, 'Where are you going?' Receiving the discourteous reply, 'Somewhere less boring,' she watched Zoe cross the road and take the path by the side of the church that led up to the spinney. Then she reached under her rug for her diary and, with satisfaction, read over her last entry. Closing it again, she glanced across to where the top of Detective Sergeant Hunter's blond head could be seen as he lounged in his garden chair. What would he think if he saw what she'd written?

Hunter was thinking of nothing very much and certainly not about Anne-Marie. With the pageant of St Oswald's life safely over and the Festal Evensong still to come, he relaxed against the canvas, soaking up the sun. He had hoped that the fifteen overs allotted to the over-twenty-fives would be completed without his services with the bat being required but his disappointment at scoring only seven runs was mitigated by twelve-year-old Tim's being chosen to open for the opposition, together with young Frank Carr. He remembered with pleasurable pride the delight in Frank's voice when he had rung him only that morning to say that Tim's prior commitment had been cancelled and he was available to play if there was still a place in the side for him. He watched idly as the two of them padded up and noticed that his son had once again appropriated his peaked driving cap from the car. Then he closed his eyes to luxuriate in this rare free Sunday and willed young Tim to cover himself with glory.

Wheezes to his right told him that Ben Poskitt, the fat landlord of the Rag and Louse, was hauling himself to his feet to follow the vicar on to the field. Opening his eyes again, he blinked at the bright sun and determined to reclaim his cap from Tim at the first opportunity. The vicar tossed the ball to Glyn Morgan. Having conferred with him about field placings, he waved to Hunter to remain just inside the boundary, within striding distance of where he had been sitting, and therefore within earshot of Frank's aside to his sister. 'Where's Zoe?'

The reply was succinct. 'Gone up the spinney. She's in a mood.'

Tim Hunter, eager to show his prowess at the wicket, pulled at

13

Frank's arm and Frank allowed himself to be led out to the middle. Hunter watched Frank carelessly take guard and instinctively play forward to a quick, short delivery from Glyn Morgan. The second was a full toss. Frank lofted it over the bowler's head into the grateful hands of Ben Poskitt.

Mr Medway was enraged. He bellowed at Frank as he left the field, 'We can tek yer wickets yer know. You don't have to offer 'em to us on a bloody plate.'

Oblivious of all censure, Frank strode off the field and towards the road that ran alongside the church. Something was amiss. Hunter followed the lad's gaze and the two of them saw Zoe emerge from the spinney into the narrow lane that led to the road. With an almost imperceptible shrug, Frank dropped back and flung himself on the grass. Hunter motioned to the vicar's brother, who had volunteered to act as twelfth man for whichever side might need one, to take his place. Swiftly he crossed the road to the white-faced girl who had stopped running as she saw him approach.

'What is it, Zoe?'

With a valiant attempt at bravado, she removed her elbow from his supporting hand and gave him a ghastly grin. 'It's the end of your weekend off. Somebody's been playing a game of murder and they've left the body behind. Oh God . . .'

Hysterical weeping had followed this flippant announcement, but with the resilience of her sixteen years Zoe had soon recovered at least sufficiently to lead Hunter back along the stony track to the small spinney where she had looked for an earring and found a particularly harrowing corpse. Once through the gap in the surrounding wall, though, her footsteps had slowed. Following her pointing finger, Hunter had made his own way through the bracken and ascertained the truth of her report.

He could well understand her reluctance. The body was that of a man. The face and hands were burned black and there was no trace of hair or clothing. The stomach and trunk were discoloured and distended and the corpse was covered in flies. He closed his eyes and swallowed several times before he was ready to face either the girl or his obligations.

Chapter 2

Returning down the track to the church at the bottom, Hunter had relinquished Zoe to her eminently sensible mother. Then he had summoned by telephone those of his superiors who would take charge of the ensuing enquiry and awaited with resignation his immediate recall to duty. He was somewhat surprised, therefore, to find himself at present, clad in royal blue cassock and white surplice, seated in the choir stalls of the church of St Oswald, just as he'd planned to be before the body was discovered. Fliss was to sing solo verses in the hymn that was the Sunday School's contribution and Hunter knew that his own strong, sweet voice was badly needed to reinforce the tenor line of the anthem. When the vicar had pleaded for the special service to go ahead as planned, even to the sergeant's participation, Hunter had held his breath. He still wasn't quite sure why acting Chief Inspector Browne had allowed it, nor why he had chosen to be part of the congregation himself. Hunter could just see him, three-quarters of the way back, standing next to Annette, his dark head bent over his open hymnbook.

The hymn finished and the congregation knelt for the Confession and Absolution. Hunter's thoughts wandered back through the weekend, and then to the vicar's announcement, in a service back in April, which had started it all off. The congregation had paid little attention, the announcement being an almost verbatim repetition of his usual one. 'Patronal festival . . . rated quite equal in this parish with the major festivals of Christmas and Easter . . . special effort in this our centenary year . . . everyone contributing his own peculiar talents . . . a truly memorable occasion.' Well, this weekend would be memorable all right. He hoped no one thought a body in the church spinney and the ensuing investigation was his contribution, introduced to display his own 'peculiar talent'. It was a particularly revolting body and Hunter could not understand why it had been left unburied. The ground was plenty soft enough with abundant leaf mould from last year.

'Come, bless the Lord all you servants of the Lord,' bellowed the aged bass standing beside him. Hunter hastily scrambled to his feet and joined in the canticle, wondering idly, as he looked around him, why the right-hand altar candle consistently burnt faster than the other. He had been commanded by Inspector Browne to report on anything in the service that was unplanned or not just as usual. There had been nothing, though, except for the insertion, by the lay reader, Gerald Morgan, of a one-sentence prayer for the repose of the soul now parted from the body outside. This petition had not been followed by the ostentatiously fervent 'Amen' with which Alan Priestley, the other reader, had favoured all the rest.

The psalm followed the canticle. 'Number eleven,' the vicar announced, 'chosen for the feast of a martyr.' Hunter stole another glance at his wife and his chief inspector, who were both giving it an enthusiastic rendering. 'He tries the righteous and the wicked: and him that delights in violence his soul abhors. He will rain down coals of fire and brimstone upon the wicked: a scorching wind shall be their cup to drink.'

This seemed to Inspector Browne a mite inconsistent on the part of the Almighty. He couldn't have it both ways. As the psalm finished and he sat down, Browne wondered if the man in the spinney had been wicked. He had certainly been visited by fire. His skin had been charred and his flesh had split open in places. In the hot, tranquil afternoon, as he had contemplated the body under the tree, the faint rustling of the leaves had seemed to add to the stillness of the tall trunk. A branch had trailed, upon which deformed and yellowing leaves mouldered, as though contaminated by the mess of human remains that they touched. Decomposition was well begun and the body had stunk beyond belief but Browne imagined that the pathologist's report would probably confirm his own opinion that death had taken place only a few days ago. The weather had caused rapid decay, and Brown had been glad. The confused turmoil of feelings that sudden death produced in him had been absent this time because the condition of this corpse made it seem less than human.

It probably had nothing whatever to do with this weekend's

16

cavortings in the church and he was finding it difficult to explain to himself exactly why he had decreed that he and his sergeant should be attenders at Evensong. He hoped he had not, but feared that he might have been motivated by a desire to humour Hunter as a means, afterwards, of getting the best out of him. But it was on the small patch of ground belonging to this institution that the body had been found. He might, therefore, usefully familiarise himself with its ritual and, for the moment, he didn't know what else to do.

Bringing his attention back to his immediate surroundings, Browne discovered that the Magnificat had begun and, as Hunter had been, he was seated among the upstanding. He felt rather than saw the disapproving glare of his sergeant's wife beside him. He had made a thorough job of embarrassing her since he had first sneaked, during the opening sentence, through the baize-covered west door. It had promised to close silently. Instead, as he gratefully tiptoed to Annette's pew, it had given a spiteful clang as it moved the last inch and juddered to a halt. No one had turned round but there had been a momentary stillness as everyone concentrated on not doing so.

He stood up hurriedly, dimly aware that he had sat through a reading from the Epistle to the Hebrews which regaled the congregation with the cruel sufferings of the faithful stalwarts of the Old Testament, 'tortured, not accepting deliverance . . . stopped the mouths of lions, quenched the violence of fire . . . turned to flight the armies of the aliens.' Whoever blamed the influence of television for violence should have a browse through this lot. And now, in the Magnificat, the congregation was busily scattering the proud in their conceit and casting down the mighty from their thrones.

When Browne realised that the next reader, having been allocated St Matthew, chapter fourteen, was about to behead John the Baptist, he had had enough slaughter and escaped once more into his own thoughts. The rest of the congregation, satisfied that this sin at least they had not committed, settled to a complacent contemplation of Salome's mother and King Herod, who had.

Browne made a mental check of the preliminary measures that had so far been taken in the investigation. The immediate area of the body had been cordoned off and the police surgeon had

17

made his statutory but otherwise superfluous certification of death, leaving the body to the joint ministrations of the Coroner's Officer and the Home Office pathologist. The latter would have dealt with the remains in situ by now and have had them removed to the lab, leaving the Scene of Crime Officers to their fingertip search of the spinney. Superintendent Petty, having seen the carrying out of his instructions under way, was probably enjoying his supper.

It had emerged that Zoe Morgan, Frank Carr and one of the readers, Alan Priestley, had walked in the spinney after last night's pageant finished. No one had so far admitted to being there after that, so Browne had arranged that the three of them and the vicar should be available for preliminary questioning after the service. He'd probably get more out of them when this church jamboree was over and their minds were free to concentrate on something else. A house-to-house enquiry had begun in the streets immediately surrounding the church and a preliminary request sent to Missing Persons with the few brief details the pathologist had been able to give them on the spot. He could think of little else that could usefully be done until these activities bore fruit or until the pathologist's full report was available.

He made himself as comfortable as he could on the buttoned cushion seat with the hard pew backrest to enjoy the rest of the proceedings. The Nunc Dimittis duly rendered, it was time for the anthem. The words, taken from the Martyr's Collect, were printed on the service sheet. 'Strengthen us with your grace, that we may endure reproach and persecution and faithfully bear witness to the name of Jesus.' The music, he learned, reading further, had been composed for this service by the choirmaster and organist who was hidden from his view behind the vicar's chair and two rows of choir stalls. Their occupants, including Hunter, rose, the organ began the introduction and Browne listened, impressed. Presently, his attention was caught by Hunter's immediate and aged neighbour, singing with every part of his anatomy, his foot tapping, his copy held out with a gesture like an Old Testament patriarch prophesying doom, mouth agape, as though only these contortions would produce the power of voice which he'd taken for granted in his younger days. He blinked back embarrassing tears at the old man's absorption in his performance. His complete unselfconsciousness was childlike and fascinated Browne. It was something he seldom achieved himself.

18

He had always a detachment, a self-awareness that prevented it. A strong, pure soprano took over the melody from the men, and Browne, startled, watched Zoe as she sang with a dedication and enjoyment that matched the old man's. He was entranced.

Suddenly, Annette leaned towards him. 'What a gross lump of a girl she is,' she whispered. 'And as hard as nails,' she added, spitefully. 'It would take more than a dead body to do that one out of her moment of glory.' Browne moved a fraction away from her to protect himself from further asides, and kept his gaze on the choir until the slight but magical piece drew to a close.

They stood and Browne's lips said the Creed as he looked around at the flower arrangements that he knew were Annette's handiwork. He found them repulsive. Each was entirely of one colour, the one on the nearest window-sill flaring orange with nasturtiums, montbretia and marigolds. The font sported a pink confection and the huge edifice in the sanctuary was all white. The blooms were defoliated and formally and stiffly arranged, their delicacy and freshness mocked by the artificial order imposed on them. This insensitive woman defiled everything she touched. A healthy bush in her garden was clipped to a ridiculous bird shape, and her engaging, gap-toothed seven-year-old was adorned with nail varnish and ear studs. How could a man of Hunter's sensibilities allow it?

On automatic pilot, Browne had put down his prayer book, found the next hymn and begun to sing it.

> 'Here as in the world around us
> All our varied skills and arts
> Wait the coming of His Spirit
> Into open minds and hearts.'

Reproved, he endeavoured to open his mind a little and to feel more tolerance for an art form for which he had not only no taste but no talent. The Lord's Prayer, versicles and responses and closing collects followed in quick succession and Browne prepared to stand whilst the choir and clergy filed out. His heart sank as they remained in their places, except for the Reverend Philip Garside, who felt he 'had to say a few words in appreciation'. The sun, on its westward journey, found its rays directed at the speaker, filtering through glass now red, now blue, now green.

The members of the Parochial Church Council, caring about the colours of neither the vicar's opinions nor his face and garments, congratulated themselves on this splendid climax to the festival they had planned and brought to pass.

At last it was over, the officiating body had departed and the congregation knelt, apparently in prayer. The organist was scribbling an improvisation on the silence and Browne was free to go. He touched Annette's shoulder, left a message for Hunter to join him in the spinney as soon as he had disrobed, then wandered outside, blinking in the bright sunshine. At seven thirty it was still very warm and sweat began to trickle between his shoulder-blades as he walked briskly up the stony lane. The sun, finding its way between the slender trunks of the trees in the gardens to his right, dappled the wall that bounded the spinney. The shrubs on the verges looked dried out, partly because the baking sun had done its worst but also because the feet that had trodden the powdery gravel of the track had kicked up a white dust that had settled on the leaves. He reached the gap that revealed the thickness of the dry stone wall of local millstone grit and passed through it to the alternate gloom and dazzle of the spinney. His feet were grateful to tread on the pungent, yielding leaf mould and he repudiated the idea of violent death in this place. The rotting corpse of an animal that had lived out its days and gone the way of all flesh was fitting but wanton destruction of vigorous life was not. The trees grew close and their proximity to each other had made the trunks and branches thin and spindly so that the blue-green bracken on the ground was more luxuriant than the foliage above. The bracken was dry and brittle too. It crumbled against Browne's trousers and fragments of it stuck to his socks. The SOCO were searching on the narrow flat area near the path but the body had been lying where the ground sloped steeply away from the church. It had probably been hidden under fronds of bracken before the fire that had disfigured it had burned its covering too.

Detective Constable Bellamy, who had watched Browne's approach, came forward clutching several small plastic bags. 'We think we've found the girl's earring, sir, under the body. Then we found a religious tract and a button. It's blue and fabric-covered and we think it's probably off a cassock, being so near the church. This bit of yellow and black polythene sheet was under

20

the leaves but it's dirty and torn. It may have nothing to do with our business. And, lastly, there's a clean, folded paper with a list of names, hand written.'

Browne peered through the plastic, trying to read the untidy scrawl on the paper, lined and torn from an exercise book, which Bellamy had unfolded before bagging it. He saw that the first name was Tim Hunter and the second Frank Carr and realised it was a list of the members of the under-twenty-five cricket team.

'The choir's cassocks are blue,' Browne volunteered. He examined the button, then the gold earring in the shape of a dolphin and the tract, printed on cheap paper in red and black and warning him that 'Verily there is a God that judges the earth'.

Bellamy looked pregnant with theories. 'Go on then,' Browne invited, 'let's hear what you've worked out so far.'

'Well, sir, could it be a professional killing? It looks as though every scrap of identification has been destroyed.' Bellamy had been nursing his idea for an hour and had it all worked out. 'No clothes on the body, the hands, especially the fingertips, burned and the face and the hair burned off so that we can't even attempt a rough sketch, never mind take a reasonable photograph.'

Browne gave the suggestion polite consideration before he refuted it. 'I don't think so. Professionals would have made an efficient job of the burning, not left a corpse with at least a few clues lying so close to a well-used path. And then, only the locals would know there's a little wood here. It's too small to be shown on a map. My first impression is that we can look fairly close to home for this job.'

Hunter had come up behind him as he spoke, dressed in his usual working attire and, for the first time that day, Browne felt comfortable with him as a colleague. Hunter, elegant in cream cricket flannels, or remote and impersonal in cassock and surplice, had not seemed a proper recipient of his preliminary musings on the case. 'Did you pick up anything from being in church, then?' he asked Browne.

The acting chief inspector raised an eyebrow at him. 'You're the one who knows what should have happened. What did you come up with?'

Hunter seemed abstracted. 'Not a lot. No one has said they've seen anything out of the way, although, apart from the choir,

21

I haven't talked to anyone. There was something funny earlier, though. Young Frank Carr, Zoe's boyfriend, was playing in the cricket match, captaining the youngsters. Every year it's keenly contested. Everyone plays to win and the lad's a good player. I believe he's been looked at for the county colts.' Hunter described how Frank had failed to notice Zoe's absence until his team's innings began, and how, on learning from his sister that she had gone to the spinney, had thrown away his wicket and been about to pursue her. Then he looked around him. 'Where's the mighty Mitchell? I'd have thought he'd be in at the kill.'

Browne was annoyed. He drew Hunter to one side. 'Constable Mitchell, if it's any of your business, is with the house-to-house lot. Give him a break, Jerry.'

Hunter sniffed but said nothing, having at least the sense to know that his resentment of the favour in which DC Mitchell stood with his acting chief inspector would, if declared, do nothing to improve the light in which Browne saw Hunter himself.

Well aware of the situation, Browne sighed and decided to deal with the annoyance by removing himself from it. 'Go and have a word with those two young folk,' he instructed Hunter. 'The vicar says you can use the church hall. Find out exactly when they walked in the spinney last night and where. I'll have a brief chat to the vicar, then I'll get back to headquarters and see if anything's come in from Missing Persons or the house-to-house people.'

They parted and Browne walked yet again down the dusty lane from the spinney to the church. The vicarage surprised him. He had expected an imposing structure of three storeys but, tucked into the far corner of the church gardens, at the side furthest from the spinney, he found a square, modern house, neat and characterless.

'They pulled down a delightful Victorian monstrosity two years ago,' Philip Garside told him as he let him in. 'Three storeys plus half-sunk cellars. A pleasure to live in in a hot August like this and a freezing horror in winter. The church commissioners have embarked on a wholesale campaign to get rid of anything that's costly to run and maintain. Even demolishing and rebuilding is considered cheaper.'

Fearing he was about to embark on a whole string of examples and give his opinion of it all, Browne began the formal interview. 'We meet in unfortunate circumstances, Mr Garside. I hope I'm

22

not in your bad books for going through the motions of worship with an ulterior motive.'

The vicar smiled and opened the door into a comfortable, untidy study. He waved Browne into a chair and settled into his own beside it. 'You were no different from the majority of the congregation. There are many kinds of church membership. I accept them all, even lip service to an undemanding deity with a sense of humour who allows worshippers to meet here on a Sunday to plan their social life for the rest of the week. It's not always politic to say so but this place would look pretty sick without them. How can I help you now?'

Browne saw that Garside was weary and as anxious as himself to avoid further small-talk. 'As you know, a young girl from your congregation found the body of a man this afternoon. He was most likely killed and we have no evidence yet to prove that it happened in the spinney, but that was where someone put him. For now, I'd like a brief description of the parish and the activities in the church and its grounds this weekend.'

Garside nodded and filled his pipe from a pouch on his desk. 'It's an interesting parish that divides itself socially in two. Up the hill from the church are solid Victorian houses, owned by respectable and well-off families, many of whom worship here – working and retired professionals. They grow and bring the flowers, polish the brass and silver and organise the church social life. Downhill and towards the town centre we have smaller terraced housing of the same period and some twentieth-century urban problems, though nothing like those in the estates on the other side of town.

'The activities here this weekend have all been to celebrate our patronal festival. August the fifth is the feast of St Oswald. We make quite a fuss about it every year, and this being our centenary, all the stops were pulled out. On Saturday afternoon the Sunday School gave a concert. On Saturday evening there was a pageant of the life of St Oswald, produced by Gerald Morgan, one of our lay readers. Today there was special singing at both services. The evening anthem was specially composed for the occasion by our organist and choirmaster.'

'I liked it,' Browne put in.

Garside looked gratified. 'Glyn is Gerald's brother. He's only a third-rank composer but certainly not third-rate. The anthem's a little gem. Alan Priestley, the other reader, preached this morning. This afternoon, as you have already been told, we had the traditional annual cricket match on the moor opposite the church.'

'A busy weekend for you.' Browne smiled sympathetically but Garside shook his head.

'But for the finding of the body, it wouldn't have been. I take overall responsibility, of course, but tradition dictates that as many people as possible take part, and there's a committee formed each year, upon which the vicar, for his sins, is not invited to sit. Your sergeant's wife was one of its leading lights this year. She was responsible for all the flower arrangements.'

Browne got hurriedly to his feet before he was obliged to express insincere admiration of them. 'That's about all at the moment, Mr Garside. I'm afraid I'll be back again when we have more idea what we're dealing with. Just one last point. We asked Zoe and Mrs Morgan to keep to themselves the details of the state of the body. Without asking you to malign your parishioners, how far would you say their assurances will be adhered to?'

The vicar smiled, widely. 'You were lucky there, Chief Inspector. I would say their adherence would be absolute.' He was ushering Browne down the hall, willing him not to prolong his departure. He offered his hand, then grimaced and let it drop as the doorbell rang. 'It's my day off tomorrow, thank goodness. I hope whatever this is doesn't take too much sorting out.'

The door opened to disclose the utterer of the fervent Amens. He wore a hand-knitted sweater against the slight cooling of the evening, puckered where the neckband had been inexpertly sewn in. The vicar looked resigned. 'Come in, Alan. I'm just seeing out Chief Inspector Browne. I'll be with you in a moment.'

As he made no movement to let Browne pass, Garside shrugged. 'This is Mr Priestley, Inspector, who preached for us this morning.'

Browne nodded and edged round the visitor who remained on the step, declaiming to himself. ' "Thy right hand shall find out those that hate thee. Thou shalt make them as a fiery oven in the time of thine anger; the Lord shall swallow them up in his wrath and the fire shall devour them." '

Browne froze on the doorstep as the vicar drew his reader inside. ' "I will turn your feasts into mourning and all your songs into lamentation." I had to come and tell you. I let that

24

poor wayward girl find the body, indecently exposed and horribly disfigured.'

Browne stepped smartly back inside. 'Excuse me, Mr Garside.' He turned and addressed the newcomer. 'When did you see the body?'

Priestley regarded him sorrowfully. 'Before the morning service, sir. I was taking my usual turn round the grounds, asking the Lord to confirm the message He'd given me for my sermon.'

Browne blinked as several new ideas struck him simultaneously. 'You found the body before the morning service?' Priestley nodded. 'Then why on earth didn't you do something about it?'

Priestley bridled, indignantly. 'I did, sir. I did!'

Chapter 3

The church tower and Gothic windows on one side of it and the well-kept-up Victorian terrace on the other made the church hall look squat and ugly in spite of its reclaimed stone facing and fresh white paint. Browne paused between the outer and inner glass doors to look at a display of snapshots taken during the playgroup's recent trip to the coast. In several of them, mothers with anxious expressions encouraged dimpled but fractious-looking toddlers to brave the edge of the waves. Browne smiled at another in which two fathers laboured with enthusiasm over a sophisticated edifice of damp sand whilst their offspring ignored them, one in tears and the other absorbed and half hidden by a huge mass of candy floss on a stick.

As he opened the inner door he walked into a wall of heat, though someone, possibly Hunter, had opened windows and drawn the curtains of those on the west side of the hall against the evening sun. He looked round. In the corner a piano stood, draped with a garish curtain of reds and purples. Those at the windows were neatly checked in green and the stacked chairs in another corner were curtained off with more green checks. Three of the chairs had been commandeered by Hunter for himself and his two witnesses. They remained, their painted tubular steel frames chipped and their wooden seats much scratched, clustered about a table, also tubular framed. Its surface, in spite of careful sandpapering, still revealed who had loved whom among the church's young people over the last few years.

The clock over the kitchen hatch had stopped at half-past one. The walls were wood-panelled and much adorned. The one allocated to the Sunday School had lists of names on charts followed by rows of stars, some long, some short, indicating perhaps that all are not equal in the sight of God.

Various doors helpfully labelled 'NO EXIT' led Browne to peer inside. One opened into a room filled with rows of minute chairs. Another, obviously the kitchen, held three efficient looking but slightly old-fashioned, non-matching cookers, given a good home in order to protect against accusations of extravagance the owners of the district's rather grand houses when they had their already convenient kitchens refitted to keep up with fashion and the inevitable Joneses.

The two young folk had been dismissed and his sergeant stood alone before a large wall decoration of blue crêpe paper, the work of the Brownies, a passable aquarium with green and silver streamers and unlikely striped and spotted paper fish. Browne indicated the uncomfortable looking chairs and they settled themselves to confer.

Hunter had managed to elicit little more from Frank and Zoe than in his preliminary interview. They had slipped out of the church hall as, the pageant finished, its audience said a protracted good night to each other, and 'walked' in the spinney together. Zoe was adamant that they had not passed by a body in the deepening dusk. They had actually sat under the tree where it had later been found. Hunter had pictured with distaste the nature of their walking and sitting. He'd make sure in a few years' time that Tim and Fliss indulged in no such vulgar behaviour. He looked up at Browne's entry and, seeing his expression, settled himself to listen.

'How well do you know the lay reader, Priestley?' Browne demanded.

Hunter looked faintly embarrassed. 'Not very. Why do you want to know about him?'

Browne looked hard at his sergeant. 'I'll come to that in a minute. Why don't you want to tell me?'

Hunter got up and wandered to the window. He stood, apparently admiring the spectacular sunset, and answered without turning. 'Rumour has it he's queer.'

Browne knew, from the set of Hunter's head and shoulders and the wave of crimson that swept over the back of his neck, that the close-set brown eyes would be narrowed and the small mouth pursed in disapproval. He sighed impatiently. He had been thankful so often for his sergeant's keen observation and intelligent deduction, but a sergeant he was destined to remain

27

until he divested himself of a mealy-mouthed embarrassment at any lack of orthodoxy and a tendency to sulk at an imagined slight. 'I'm not sure that's relevant. What I chiefly want to know is, is he off his head?'

Hunter considered. 'There are people who would say so. They're mostly the ones who don't go along with his theology, if that's the word for the things he believes.'

'I take it you don't then.'

On less uneasy ground now, Hunter turned back into the room. 'Not entirely, although a lot of the opposition to what he says is because of its unpalatable truth. He has a very simplistic view of God, man and everything else, but I definitely wouldn't say he was off his head. Why?'

Hunter's eyes widened as Browne dropped his bombshell and described the rest of his recent encounter with Priestley. 'He decided that, since nothing could be done for the victim, it would be a pity to start a furore that might put a stop to the church celebrations. "The Lord's work must always come first." His method of dealing with the situation was to keep an eye on any youngsters who might have strayed into the spinney and head them off. Oh – and he decided to drop a religious tract beside the body for the spiritual benefit of the officiating police. He asked, most particularly, whether anyone had read it and was gratified that many of us had. It supported his theory that the Lord always brings good out of evil! He assured me he fully intended to report to us after the evening service, and he apologised most profusely, not for holding up the enquiry but for letting young Zoe escape his vigilance and receive such a nasty shock.'

Before the narrative had finished, Hunter was smiling. 'Sounds fairly typical. He thinks quite logically according to his lights. Anyway, so much for Exhibit A.'

Browne grinned. 'Well, it's gone to the lab with the rest of the gubbins now. By the way, has Priestley any particular partner? His religious leanings don't suggest he's a one-night-stand man.'

Hunter's lips tightened. 'He took in a student type a week or two back. He came to church with Priestley for a while, though I haven't seen him for the last couple of Sundays.'

Browne considered, then made for the door, pausing as he reached it. 'So you haven't seen enough of them to know whether they're fond of one another?'

Hunter flushed again. 'Well, I presume they must be.'

Browne searched his pockets for his keys. 'Not necessarily. It might be a convenient mutually satisfying . . .'

'No, I haven't seen enough of them,' Hunter put in hurriedly.

Browne triumphantly produced his keys from the folds of a handkerchief that had stifled their jingling. 'Well, I shall have to find someone who has. I'll have to find a better reason than he's given me for failing to report a murder. In the meantime, starting with Annette, set your ear to the ground and see what you can pick up about the younger partner. There's nothing more we can do tonight, Jerry. I suggest we let the long-suffering verger lock up this place and call in at HQ to see if anything has come in. If, as I anticipate, there's zilch, we'll go home to bed. There'll be plenty to do tomorrow.'

As Browne climbed into his car, he was actually looking forward to his early night. Only as he drove alongside the moor in the direction of home did he remember the family argument which the call to the spinney had interrupted. It was the third or fourth on the same subject and it wouldn't be the last. And he had a growing feeling that he wasn't going to win it. Perhaps some sort of compromise was the best answer. Virginia wouldn't be eighteen until the end of the month. Even if she capitulated and accepted the university place she had been offered – provided, of course, that her A level results were up to scratch – perhaps she was rather young to take full advantage of the opportunities there. Perhaps he'd suggest that she took a year out and ask for her place to be held open for next year. He knew it was putting off the problem, not resolving it, and sighed as he remembered the days when his children had been small and biddable. Never mind. Maybe Virginia would be out when he arrived home and he wouldn't have to face Round Five till another day.

In his dining room on Monday morning, Browne chatted briefly with his wife over breakfast. The unreasonable monster with whom he had wrangled the previous afternoon had inexplicably been replaced by the daughter he knew and loved. She was making extra toast in the kitchen and calling through her plans for the day. She was to spend it helping with a holiday project, supervising and occupying a group of handicapped youngsters. She had originally done this work to obtain a service flash as

29

part of the Duke of Edinburgh Award scheme, but because of her enthusiasm for the cause and her fondness for the children, she had offered her services every summer since.

'You'd have laughed at James yesterday,' she called, but her anecdote was interrupted by a small scream and an acrid smell. Browne grinned. 'How many years have you been going to Dean Royd now?' he asked her as he accepted his burnt offering with good grace.

'Four.' The tip of her tongue emerged from the side of her mouth as she concentrated on using the butter to stick together her brittle fragments of overdone toast.

Browne pushed his plate to one side, rose and began gathering the impedimenta of a day's work in preparation for his departure. 'You really enjoy it, don't you?' he asked approvingly, heading for the door.

She eyed him, speculatively. 'Well, that's why I've gone on doing it but it'll be useful now. It's going to look good on the form when I apply to join the Specials.'

Browne felt he had been hit below the belt. He had thought that the desire to establish at least a temporary truce on the subject of his daughter's future had been mutual.

'Your father's in a rush. You can talk to him about that when he comes home,' her mother put in hurriedly. He took the hint and continued his progress down the hall. He was sure, as he turned away, that Virginia and Hannah had exchanged a wink.

Arriving at the station, Browne found the incident room humming busily. He decided to retire to his office to read through the preliminary reports and then spoil the Reverend Philip Garside's day off by consulting him about the personality and mental balance of the more evangelical of his lay readers. He started with a cup of coffee and the single sheet sent over from Missing Persons. The information it contained was too general to be useful, which was hardly surprising when the only two firm facts about the victim he had sent them were that he was male and dead. He relinquished it for Hunter's perusal whilst he examined the SOCO report.

A couple of constables hovered outside his open door, hopeful of gleaning some interesting clue. Browne issued the hoped-for invitation but made them wait until he had drained his cup and laid down the report. 'The search of the spinney served the useful

30

purpose of clearing a great deal of litter,' he informed them, 'but there seems no reason to associate any particular piece of it with the body. Mr Priestley has explained the tract to us and there's no particular significance in Zoe's earring being found under the body, since she told you' – nodding in Hunter's direction – 'that she and her gentleman friend sat on that comfortable patch of bracken on Saturday night.'

'She'd taken them off and put them in her pocket,' Hunter volunteered.

'Well, they are uncomfortable to wear if you're sitting down in a wood,' Mitchell put in, grinning lasciviously.

Hunter quelled him with a glare and addressed Browne again. 'Zoe's probably responsible for the cassock button too. One of her father's came off during choir practice on Friday evening. She put it in her pocket intending to sew it on for him but she couldn't find it last night.'

'Her father? Glyn Morgan? Choirmaster and organist – and composer, according to last night's programme?' Hunter nodded. 'Right, for the moment we won't follow up every last sweet and cigarette packet. What's come in from the house-to-house?'

The substance of Mitchell's answer was sufficiently trivial and irrelevant for Hunter to feel a snub was not required, especially as the constables were immediately despatched to continue their assault on the doors of the surrounding streets. Hunter himself was assigned to an hour of tedious paperwork and Browne made for the car park and his visit to St Oswald's vicarage. As he reached the main entrance, he was surprised and pleased to see the pathologist, Ledgard, striding towards him. He greeted him hopefully. 'They're not fitting it in today?'

The grizzled auburn head nodded once. 'You're in luck. I didn't think we ever had a slack time but chummy's the only one in. Coming in my car?'

'I'd better follow in mine. I need to be back as soon as possible. Garside will get his morning off after all.'

When he returned to the station later that morning, Browne saw Hunter in the middle distance and motioned him to come into his office. After making him earn the privilege by sending him in search of more coffee, he shared with his sergeant the results of the autopsy as far as they were known. 'Right then, we have a male, early forties, good health. Considering the hot weather he probably died four to five days ago. Petrol was used for burning but not enough of it or the body would have been reduced to ashes. Some of the fingers may still be sufficiently intact to take some prints. The lab's struggling with it now.'

'And the cause of death?'

Browne shrugged. 'No external injuries. Ledgard's sent samples to the HO lab. Oh – and about three weeks ago someone did something called a wedge resection on the nail of the big toe on his left foot. Not Zadeck's operation. That would mean cutting into the nail bed and would need a general anaesthetic.' Hunter looked startled until he realised that Browne was reading from his notebook. 'The resection was probably done in a hospital but we'd better check GPs as well. Some of them would do it in the surgery. Get back to Missing Persons, Jerry, and give them the details we've got now.'

'Right.' Hunter strode out into the corridor and towards the incident room. Browne remained, elbows on his desk, staring unseeing at its surface and assimilating the facts he had just received. The most promising was the minor surgery to the toe. He had noticed that it seemed to have sustained some injury but now he had the precise terminology he could ask the hospitals some specific questions.

A tap at his door preceded the appearance of Mitchell. Broad-shouldered, bullet-headed and barely regulation height, the lad stood, thick lips parted, his expression eager, waiting for permission to speak. Browne contemplated him with mixed feelings, welcoming his diligence and astuteness on the case. What he lacked in experience he made up for with quick thinking and enthusiasm. On the other hand, the mutual antipathy between him and Hunter was irritating, and Browne suspected that a preference for his company had at least a little to do with Virginia's adamant refusal to be packed off to Oxford in the autumn. Mitchell hovered in the doorway until Browne invited him in.

'There's a Mrs Smithson, sir, from Ings Lane. Her husband's at work till two o'clock. A railway guard on mornings. She says he was awake a chunk of Saturday night with toothache. Ings Lane backs on to the track that runs alongside the spinney. He says there was a car parked by the gap in the wall just after midnight and people getting out. He didn't go to the window but the curtains were drawn back and he saw the lights and heard the doors slam. He thinks whoever got out may have opened the boot – he heard low voices and another slam. He doesn't know how long the car was there because he made a hot drink and went through to the front room.'

The phone on Browne's desk rang once. Browne lifted the receiver, listened, said 'Thanks' and replaced it. 'That was Hunter. No person reported missing corresponds to our corpse. Penny for them, Mitchell.'

A look of intense concentration had replaced Mitchell's habitual smirk. 'I was thinking of what sort of people could be missing but not missed.'

'And what have you come up with?'

Mitchell took the seat that Browne indicated. 'Well, commercial travellers, people going round looking for work. Or it could be somebody living on his own that nobody cared about or got to know.'

'Somebody knew him,' Browne rejoined, 'or why kill him?'

Mitchell sat forward. 'What if he was a salesman, carrying something a bit valuable? And suppose he picked up a hitcher who robbed him and killed him, then drove him in his own car till he happened to pass the spinney. He could have dumped him and poured the reserve can of petrol over him, set him on fire and cleared off. It'd be easy to get rid of the car to a crooked dealer – or he could have pushed it into a lake somewhere.'

Browne was amused. 'No marks on the body. Any theories about what method your hitch-hiker used?'

Mitchell looked eager rather than embarrassed. 'Have we got a PM report already, sir?'

His eyes pleaded for information and Browne threw him a few scraps. 'Fortyish, good health and a sizeable chunk neatly and professionally cut out of the nail of his big toe.'

Another tap at the door produced Hunter who darted a malevolent look at Mitchell. The constable stiffened and deliberately looked away. Browne was angry. They could both learn to live and work together in a civilised fashion or they could both get out of his team. He was more annoyed with Hunter who was old enough and should have been experienced enough to know better.

Mitchell spoke, much more diffidently now. 'I suppose we check with the hospitals, sir?'

'You two do. Ring all the ones in Cloughton, Bradford and Leeds for a start. Divide the list between you and, as Dr Ledgard thinks that most self-respecting GPs could have done it in their surgeries, you'd better ring them as well. Ask them to go back four weeks.' He glared at them both as they departed in silence, amused that his displeasure had caused Hunter to accept dismissal without saying why he had come. Now that Mitchell was busy with the telephone, he chose Bellamy to interview the railway guard. When he'd arranged that he'd have deserved lunch – nothing too substantial or he'd fall asleep over the mound of paperwork he intended to do as he waited for further reports to come in.

When a tedious afternoon had brought in nothing, he decided to allow himself the luxury of an evening meal at home at a conventional time. Nothing, he determined, would be said about boyfriends, the Specials or university courses.

For more than an hour this was managed, chiefly because Virginia, having eaten hurriedly and excused herself, retired to her bedroom to make such adjustments to her appearance as were necessitated by the prospect of an evening out with DC Benedict Mitchell. By the time he arrived to collect her, Browne and Hannah were in hot dispute.

As he had expected, Hannah took Virginia's part. 'She's eighteen in three weeks' time, Tom.'

'Yes, and behaves half the time like a retarded twelve.' He was shocked himself at the unfairness of this and Hannah scorned to challenge it. 'She's very responsible for the other half,' he offered, lamely.

'Your assessment of her degree of maturity, accurate or not, doesn't enter into it.' Hannah deftly stowed away the débris from their meal in appropriate places. 'This time next month she'll be legally of age. If she wants to finish with formal education, we can't stop her and she'll get very little out of a university course if she's chock full of resentment about being there.'

She glanced out of the window as the doorbell rang and Virginia's feet thundered in the hall. Browne joined her and regarded his daughter through the pane with some complacency. She was taller than both himself and Mitchell. Her dark hair, cut very short, curled neatly round her ears but she had made her usual effort to look scruffy. He chuckled. 'She looked tidier before she got ready. I must say Benny's looking smart.'

Hannah slipped her hand through his arm. 'I should think the tie and jacket are more to soften you up than to impress Ginny.' They watched indulgently as the young folk, arms round each other's waists, wandered towards the gate. Mitchell opened it for Virginia and closed it behind her.

'Showing Daddy your nice manners?' She ran to avoid the smack he aimed at her.

He caught her up and took her hand. 'Rag and Louse all right?'

She nodded. 'So long as you're not listening in to hear whether other drinkers are describing how they dumped a body in the spinney.' They walked companionably the half mile to the pub.

'Sure you don't want to go somewhere miles from Ossie's?'

She shook her head. 'This is fine. We won't sit in the same alcove as the vicar! I'm glad you weren't late, Benny. Mum and Dad were going at it hammer and tongs when you arrived.'

He looked startled. 'Aren't they getting on? I'm sorry about that.'

Virginia laughed. 'They're getting along fine. My parents argue like other people play Snakes and Ladders. They go all out and when one of them wins they put the game away and get on with the rest of life. It's just that they were arguing about me – whether I should go off to Oxford in October.' They found an empty table and Mitchell removed his jacket. 'Mum's on my side and says I can always do a degree later if I change my mind. Dad thinks because Alex is there I have to go too. I've a sneaking suspicion he's afraid that if I don't go people will say he doesn't believe in educating girls.'

'Is Alex at Oxford?'

Virginia felt in the pocket of her jeans and produced a five pound note. 'No, Durham. And it's my turn to pay. Don't argue, Benny, or we won't go out again.'

Mitchell obediently took the money and came back bearing half pint tankards, hoping Virginia wouldn't comment. 'I don't mind fetching that cat's pee so much when you've paid for it yourself.' He pushed the lager towards her and sampled his own bitter.

'Don't be vulgar. It doesn't go with the tie and the nice boy image.'

He sighed and leaned across the table to look at her. 'Is that what your parents' row was about? Your association with a vulgar, menial DC when you could have an Oxford student with a brilliant career ahead of him?'

She shook her head impatiently. 'I've told you. It wasn't a row. And you ought to know Dad better than to think he expects me to find a boyfriend with high connections. They probably think you're one of the reasons I won't move away though. It's all rolled into one really, university and you and the Specials. Dad wants me to stay a schoolgirl and, since that's impossible, he's trying to settle for me being a student instead.'

Mitchell dropped his gaze and lifted the tankard again. 'And am I? – The reason you won't go?'

She shook her head again. 'Not really. Oxford isn't the other end of the earth and we can both drive. Let's talk about something else. Why did you have to go to the library when you came off duty?'

'To read up all about poisons.'

Her eyes widened. 'Whatever for?'

'Leave it off, Ginny,' he muttered. 'It's only an idea of mine and I shouldn't have said that much.'

She understood his position, but almost eighteen years of being a policeman's daughter had not cured her of finding a murder hunt riveting. She ruminated on the hint Mitchell had let fall as she finished her drink. The pub was growing stuffy and when Mitchell, too, had set down his empty tankard she proposed a walk along the canal bank.

Hannah had also suggested the canal bank as a pleasant place to enjoy the cool of the early evening but Browne had demurred. He never had enough spare time to tire of the delights of his own back garden and, in any case, the canal was where he suspected his daughter might be found. He was quite sufficiently at odds with her, without raising the suspicion of his spying on the manner in which she conducted herself with his detective constable.

Hannah, quite seeing his point, chose a record from the cabinet. Strains of Shostakovich filled the living room and Browne was thankful for the telephone that rescued him. He took the call in his little study under the stairs. Eight big toe nails had been resectioned by the recipients of their enquiries, only five on left feet and only three of those on males of approximately the right age. 'None of them seems to be at home,' Hunter's voice informed him. Browne stretched in his chair, feeling slightly guilty. 'Right. You've earned your supper, Jerry. Go and read Fliss a bedtime story and we'll try them again in the morning.'

At nine o'clock on Tuesday morning Browne stood outside the partly opened door of the incident room, reluctant to interrupt what seemed to be a seminar on criminal psychology.

'You mean murderers are born different from other people?' Bellamy's voice asked.

'People capable of murder are,' announced Richard Dean, confidently. 'People with an absolute obsession about being in the right. There's a personality type that's quite incapable of self-criticism and which can't cope with criticism from other people either. You must have met the sort of bloke who thinks he can do what he likes but his wife and children, and even his friends, have to do what he tells them. There's always a violent reaction if his authority is challenged or he is confronted with his own inadequacies.'

Browne grinned to himself. The cocky detective constable was all of twenty-seven and he had more than half an idea which book Dean had been reading.

Hunter's voice chimed in. 'I don't agree. I think, under sufficient stress, anyone might react violently and even kill. Most murders are unintentional.' Now Hunter was becoming dogmatic. 'They aren't carefully planned for material gain or for revenge, except in stories. Even nowadays, when almost anything goes, killers have too much to lose. Anyway, no one feels as strongly as that about anything any more.'

'They do about some things.' This was Mitchell. At his suggestive tone, Browne could imagine the expression of distaste on Hunter's face. 'And, anyway,' he continued, determined to antagonise Hunter further, 'our body was probably poisoned. You're not telling me the customer we're after just happened to have the wherewithal in his pocket and that he got annoyed and rammed it down his victim's throat before he could stop himself?' He seemed to have forgotten the rather similar theory that he had advanced to his chief inspector only a few days ago.

Browne agreed however that it was high time to return to the case in hand, and pushed the door fully open as Dean remarked, 'Poison's supposed to be a woman's weapon – or a doctor's.' Another attempt to display his wide reading, Browne wondered, or a bid to pour oil on troubled waters by changing the subject slightly?

'A knowledge of the properties of poisons does suggest a certain mental ability,' Hunter added, pompously. 'Some famous poisoners have belonged to the educated classes.'

'Educated enough to be able to read "Poison" on a label?' The aggressive tone was not a fitting one for a detective constable to use in addressing a detective sergeant. Mitchell realised he had gone too far and meekly accepted the rebuke Browne administered.

The group gathered round the inspector for instructions. Throwing the antagonists together yesterday didn't seem to have achieved very much so Browne decided today he would keep them apart. The two of them and Dean he despatched severally to interview the three patients so far reported by one hospital and one surgery to have been treated for an ingrowing toe nail.

Chapter 4

Hunter trudged along a street of small, terraced houses whose front doors opened directly on to the pavement, walking past the dark green paint and glass panels of number twelve to assure himself that this really was Smithson Street. Having checked with the black and white sign below the bedroom window of the end house, he retraced his steps and paused in front of the residence of Mr Norman Jackson. Its paint was recent, unscarred but also unwashed. Mr Jackson, Hunter decided, was a bachelor. His house seemed in good repair but it lacked a woman's care and concern. And this would be an abortive visit to it because if his remains were not lying in the path lab he would probably be out at work. He shrugged his shirt and jacket until they settled more comfortably on his sticky shoulders, then rapped on the dusty reeded glass.

To his relief he saw colours and movement through it and the door was opened by a brassy blonde woman with sharp features and a cigarette in her fingers. Her eyes took in the almost six and a half feet of him and the chill of his disapproval, and she evidently decided, whatever his business, that she would keep him on the doorstep.

Hunter pulled the front of his collar away from his damp neck. 'Mrs Jackson?'

She tossed her head. 'You wouldn't catch her round here. One of those posh places along by St Ossie's is her stamping ground.'

Hunter looked startled. 'Isn't this Mr Norman Jackson's house?'

'That isn't what you asked. Yes, it's Norman's place. I'm what the law calls his common-law wife – Shirley Potter.'

Hunter tried to swallow his distaste for her and appear approachable. 'And I'm what you call the law. May I come in for a minute?'

Scenting trouble for the more favourably placed wife she relented but remained on the doorstep until she had addressed an indignant glare at the cobbled street. 'I suppose so, unless you want to stay out here and have tea on the lawn.' She smiled bitterly as she let him into the sordidly untidy living room. 'I thought, when I persuaded Nor to divorce her, that I'd be living on the swanky side of town and she'd clear off with her fancy man, not that he'd move in there with her as bold as brass and Nor too daft to stop it. In trouble with the fuzz are they?'

Hunter shook his head. 'I wouldn't know. It was Mr Jackson I wanted to see.'

Her antagonism returned. 'Well he's done nothing wrong. He hasn't the gorm. How he ever got his degree and his teaching job I shall never know. He hasn't a ha'p'orth of common sense or push about him.'

'Where is he?'

She blinked as Hunter cut her short and looked sulky. 'He's gone off back to the university, if you must know. Some place down south called Keele. When he got started on his teaching he didn't like it but she thought it was a respectable job with security and she wouldn't let him leave it. The kids ran riot round him. Anyway, this Keele place is running a course for people who want to change from teaching, telling them other ways they could earn a living.'

'Did he attend the Infirmary three weeks ago to have an operation on his big toe nail?'

The woman looked astonished at Hunter's omniscience. 'Yes, he did. A right mess it was, all septic and yellow.'

'I see. Good. I hope your – er – Mr Jackson finds his course helpful.'

Having given him most of the information he wanted, Miss Potter was becoming friendly. 'Shall I make you some tea – or would you like something stronger?'

Hunter looked round at the evidence of her feckless housekeeping and repressed a shudder at the thought of her kitchen. On the piano, standing between a cup and saucer containing dried coffee grounds and an overflowing ashtray, was a framed photograph. He avoided refusing her offer by distracting her. 'Is that Mr Jackson?'

She nodded. In the picture the man was leaning over another

40

piano, probably in a pub. One huge, stubby-fingered hand held the lid, the other rested lightly on the keys. Brawny arms stretched the ribbed cuffs of his short sleeves. His shirt, buttons strained to accommodate his huge stomach, was open at the neck, revealing powerful throat muscles. Hunter guessed he played to accompany his own roaring bass. The face was fleshy, its smile indicating an easy-going cheerfulness. The ruddy complexion was topped by grey hair but the bushy brows were still dark. He looked, Hunter considered, as though he deserved better than this woman. He looked, too, as though he would accept philosophically whatever conditions he found, rather than go bustling off on redirectional courses. Hunter decided to check whether he really was at Keele University. It was certainly difficult, though, to picture him in a classroom.

Feeling more than usually grateful for Annette's fastidious housekeeping he took his leave. As he paused by his car to locate his keys in the depths of his pocket, he was comforted to observe that most of the rest of the tiny houses in the street shone with their owners' pride in them. He set off back to the station to make his phone call and check 'the posh places along by St Ossie's'. Mrs Jackson was possibly a member of the congregation and almost certainly familiar with the spinney.

Dean found himself in more salubrious surroundings. He had persuaded the police Escort along a winding road that tacked its way up the precipitous valley side to the point where the town had run out of safe ledges on which to perch more buildings and given up its struggle to extend. There he discovered that Sorland Heights was an attractive terrace of stone cottages, divided into narrow dwellings, all well cared for with fresh paint and colourful gardens. Walking along the row he found they had only gates with neat numbers, until he reached the three at the far end. From the devastation caused by knocking down their dividing walls, an imposing house was emerging. He had found Owl Cottage.

He walked slowly round it, examining it back and front. When it was finished, calling it a cottage would be an affectation. The work in progress was more a rebuilding than a renovation but it was in keeping with the rest of the terrace, retaining the grey slate roofing. What had been long narrow gardens was, at the moment, a wasteland of baked earth and builders' rubble, except

41

for one shrub, carefully avoided and preserved. Dean failed to recognise the species but admired its glossy dark leaves and its budding promise of huge white blooms. Glancing up at two tiny attic windows, he noticed that ancient stone guttering extended beyond the gable end, making it look uncannily like the ears of an enormous owl. The attic windows glinted in the sun, winking at him and enhancing the effect. Dean mentally withdrew his objection to the house's name and decided that Mr John Roberts, unless his remains had recently been removed from the spinney, would be a gentleman with a sense of humour.

He walked round to the front again, picking his way through the rubble, and knocked on the only door which had been retained. It was opened by a workman in a torn, short-sleeved shirt and dungarees. Dean looked beyond him and saw a beautifully proportioned hall in which the exposed beams and open fireplace of the living room it had been were still featured. He nodded approvingly. 'You're doing a good job here,' he told the workman patronisingly. 'I bet it cost the owner a pretty penny.'

The workman eyed him coolly. 'I don't take bets. Can I help you in some way?'

The cultured voice and clipped tone told Dean he had blundered. He showed the man his credentials. 'Are you Mr Roberts?' He looked again at the face above the stained and dusty denim and saw that this was no builder's labourer. The glance was blue and keen, the nose long and thin and mouth and chin were hidden by a moustache and full beard, both neatly trimmed and dark-going-grey like his hair. The skin was sun-tanned but it was not really an outdoor face.

The man nodded in a not unfriendly fashion and Dean hastened to retrieve the situation and ingratiate himself. 'Is this your line, sir, interior decoration and design?'

Roberts took a step backwards. 'Do you mind if I carry on for a few minutes? I'll listen to you but I've just mixed a new lot of plaster and I'd like to slap it on before it hardens.'

Dean indicated consent and followed him inside. Roberts was already busy and answered the question with his back turned. 'If you're asking whether this is my trade, no, it isn't. It is my obsession, though. Not this conversion in particular but beautiful things in general. I'm a butcher by trade.' Dean was astonished. 'I started with a market stall in Huddersfield and now I've two shops there, three in Bradford and one here in Cloughton.'

Dean made the connection, realised he knew it well and hastened to assure Mr Roberts that his mother was a regular customer.

Roberts, however, had returned to his first theme. 'I don't collect them – beautiful things, I mean. That's selfish and pointless. I find where they are and enjoy them there. Or else I try to make them. When I first bought up these three cottages there was a lot of ill-feeling from the other owners but they've come round now they've seen I'm not a vandal and they pop in to offer advice.'

As he paused to draw breath, Dean took out his notebook to recall Roberts's attention to the official nature of his visit. Roberts listened, then produced his driving licence and his neatly bandaged toe for Dean's inspection. 'It doesn't really need a bandage any more. It's healing well but I thought I'd better keep all this plaster dust off it. I'm pleased to assure you that I'm not your unfortunate victim.'

Mitchell set off quite cheerfully. Hunter had been included in the fagging usually reserved for mere constables and all he'd done to deserve it was to suffer a constable's bad manners. He had begun at a brisk pace, but the discomfort of his streaming brow and sticky underarms soon slowed him. The bright sunlight lifted his mood, though, and lent colour to the heather-clad hillside that reared up close behind the tall Victorian buildings in the bottom of the valley. The town always reminded him of Greendale, in the cartoon his little sister had watched as a child, through which Postman Pat drove his little red van. It looked as though, if he climbed to the town hall roof, he could lean over and pluck bracken from the ground that rose behind it, and traffic seemed to bounce over hills as ridiculously and abruptly steep.

He had tried again this morning to raise Gary Carr on the telephone but there had still been no answer. Was he missing? Had they found the corpse's identity already? He found Burnley Brow with no difficulty and checked again that there was no one in at number nineteen. Nor at seventeen nor twenty-one. He looked about him. It was the sort of area his mother would have described as 'very select'. She would have considered the yellow sandstone of the houses and bungalows to be in better

43

taste than the functional red brick of the council estate where she had reared him. And 'select' was apposite in a way. The houses were small but all their inhabitants had chosen them. Their gardens and general maintenance showed their pride and pleasure in them. Some of the gardens on Mitchell's parents' estate featured modern sculpture comprising disused rusty prams and old bicycles. In the garden opposite a woman was tidying plants that trailed from a plastic urn. She looked up as he approached her.

'Were you looking for Mrs Carr? Her mother's not worse is she?'

Mitchell leaned on the wall to enjoy the scent of the lavender hedge. 'Not so far as I know. I'm looking for Mr Carr, actually.'

She came to the wall to join him and Mitchell, acutely aware of the faint odour from his armpits, backed away as far as politeness allowed.

'He's still away, I think,' the woman volunteered. 'Working down south somewhere to help out a friend, so Anne-Marie was telling me. Went some time on Tuesday.'

'Who's Anne-Marie?'

The woman looked harder at him. 'You're not a friend of theirs, then?' Her tone was suspicious.

Mitchell sighed and showed her his warrant card. 'I just need a word with him. I've never met him.'

She now felt free to sniff as a sign that Mitchell had not suffered any privation, and he watched her battle with her natural curiosity. She won and asked no further questions. 'You'd better have a word with Mrs Carr, then. Theresa she is. Anne-Marie's the daughter. She's at work just now at the surgery.'

'She's a doctor?' Desirable though the houses were compared with his own, Mitchell had thought medical practitioners would live in greater luxury.

'No, she's some sort of receptionist, though the airs she gives herself, you'd think she knew more than they do. She asks more questions when you go there at any rate.' She realised she was sinking to vulgar gossip and smiled ruefully. 'I expect she's paid to protect them from time-wasters. Anyway, if it's urgent, that's where you'll find her. It's round the corner in Crossley Close.'

Mitchell recognised the address of the GP who had performed the operation on Carr's toe. 'That's Dr Fenwick?'

She nodded and again bit back the curious questions that

respectable neighbours didn't ask. 'That's right. I hope Mrs Carr can help you.' She returned to pulling single blades of grass from between the petunias in the urn. Mitchell set off in the direction the woman had indicated, wondering whether, when he had made his enquiry, he dared nip home for a shower.

He decided he'd better not and was given his reward, though with ill grace, when he arrived back at the station, having carried out his instructions as far as possible. 'I hope you're still watching your tongue,' Browne warned him. Then, lightening his tone, 'Go and wash the lather off and we'll review progress over coffee in my office.' He was not overly concerned for Mitchell's physical comfort but suspected he would make a more wholehearted effort if he were not preoccupied with fears for his personal freshness. Ten minutes later, the constable presented himself, cooler and grateful. He accepted his cup, retired with it to the smaller of the two armchairs and watched the bubbles that rose following the submersion of two sugar lumps.

Browne summarised the investigations carried out by Dean and Hunter. 'Sergeant Hunter's now busy phoning Keele University to make sure that Jackson actually arrived and is still with them. What about Gary Carr?'

Mitchell smoothed his still-damp hair, regretting that he had not been able to give it its usual blow-dry. 'I have to double-check as well. Carr's apparently a mechanic, when he works. He'd lost a job at a garage in Bradford a couple of months ago and last week was rung up by a garage-owning friend in Harlow who asked if he could go down and take the place of one of his men who'd had a road accident. The friend had a lot of jobs booked in and was desperate so Carr set off as soon as he was ready on Tuesday night.'

Browne nodded. 'Right. You'd better check that as soon as you've drunk up.'

Mitchell shook his head. 'No, I can't. The wife has no address or telephone number and only knows the first name of the friend. Apparently, whilst she was busy packing some clothes for Carr, her mother rang to say she wasn't well. Mrs Carr popped over to check on her and found her in the throes of some sort of mild heart attack and she had to be taken to hospital. She didn't get home until after her husband had gone off to catch the train, the nine fifty-eight from Bradford. He hadn't left her any way of getting in touch with him but she supposed he'd ring.'

45

'But he didn't?' Browne asked, hopefully.

'Yes, he did. Said he was working all hours to catch up on the backlog of jobs so the call was brief. He said he was comfortably settled in with his mate and didn't know when he'd be back but it probably wouldn't be long. Then he rang off. She didn't seem very concerned. Said he was always a bit casual and everything had happened in such a rush.'

Browne wrinkled his nose. 'Sounds odd. When was this phone call?'

'Sunday morning about eleven.'

Hunter's entry prevented any elaboration on this answer. The sergeant declined a chair, seized his coffee cup, fastidiously removed a trace of skin from the cooling liquid and retired to the window. 'Jackson's OK,' he said, over his shoulder. 'He arrived at Keele two days ago and is still there. He was brought to the phone to speak to me, furious because my enquiries had put the wind up his woman and she'd got in before me and been giving him earache.'

Browne summarised Mitchell's report, whilst Hunter, his luke-warm coffee abandoned, paced the office, listening. Seeing his expression, Browne broke off, an eyebrow raised in question.

'I know Gary Carr.' He dropped into the fat armchair. 'He attends St Oswald's occasionally. His wife's a pillar of the place.'

Browne beamed. His attendance at evensong had been vindicated. 'I'll let Mitchell finish the tale. It's a bit odd.'

Mitchell took it up and as he finished, Hunter frowned. 'Why did he ring her on Sunday morning? He wouldn't have expected her to be in. She's in church every week, come hail, rain or tempest.'

Browne sat forward eagerly. 'Are you telling me she's lying? That she was at morning service at that time?'

'Well, no, she wasn't. Apparently she'd passed out during breakfast and wasn't fit.' He took another turn round the office as he recapitulated the events of Sunday morning.

Browne swivelled his chair to face him. 'Could he have heard that she was ill? Rung because of it?'

Hunter shook his head. 'Presumably no one else knew where this temporary employer lived if Theresa didn't. There are two teenage children but if they knew they'd have told her. The boy was the youngster who walked with Zoe in the spinney.'

46

'Where were they when the phone message came?' Mitchell asked.

Hunter pondered. 'Both in church, I think. The boy read a lesson so I'm sure about him.'

'Wouldn't the girl have stayed at home if her mother was ill?'

Hunter shrugged. 'She wouldn't have been a lot of use if she had. She's fifteen but you'd never think so.'

'A bit backward, you mean?'

Hunter struggled to define his impression. 'Not exactly. Undeveloped, immature. Still a little girl. Nothing wrong with her mind, though. I think she does quite well at school.' He turned back, suddenly, to Browne. 'Just a minute, she was in church. She went forward with the Sunday School children to sing their hymn. The next oldest child must have been younger than Tim and I couldn't imagine him tripping out to be a sunbeam with the tinies. I remember wondering how long it would be before she wanted to dissociate herself from them.'

'When I went to the house,' Mitchell put in, 'the dolly bird across the road thought I'd come with bad news about Mrs Carr's mother.'

Hunter grimaced. 'As far as the family's concerned the bad news would be that the old woman was making a good recovery. Old-fashioned, domineering matriarch.'

Browne stood up. 'We'd better look into all this. Jerry, it might be an idea if you had a word with the youngsters as a family friend. If you mix your questions with enquiries after their grandmother's health and how their father's liking his stay in Essex it shouldn't put Mrs Carr's back up too much.'

Hunter was doubtful. 'I like her well enough but she knows what I think of her work-shy soul mate. She doesn't consider me sympathetic.'

'All right, you can start from the other end. Get on to the Harlow police, give them what little we've got and see what they can come up with.'

He dismissed them with a nod, but Hunter hesitated in the doorway. 'Do you think it would be wise, sir, to widen the search for people who might have done that toe? I don't think any more than you do that Gary Carr is beavering away in Harlow in order to shower luxuries on his family, but that doesn't make him our corpse. It's quite likely that he's just skipped for reasons of his

47

own. He's not fond of either responsibility or criticism and he was getting a fair amount of flak from young Frank. The lad didn't see why his mother should be both home-maker and sole breadwinner. He's bright and hopes to go off to university next year, but he feels guilty about not earning himself and the burden it throws on Theresa.'

Browne smiled grimly. 'You mean he actually sees some point in further education? Perhaps you'll introduce him to Ginny. You've made a good point, though. We shouldn't let the trail go cold on the right man when we could still be chasing the wrong one. I'll put Dean and Bellamy on to it. Did you mean she knows he's made off and is covering up for him or that he's put someone up to calling him away to fool her? And wouldn't it be simpler just to walk out?'

Hunter shrugged. 'Depends whether he might want to come back again. I only suggest either as a possibility.' He closed the door behind him.

A deep gloom settled over Browne, which he recognised as the inevitable prospect of more paperwork. Its only cure was the despatching of it with the resultant glow of self-approbation. He settled down to it but was pleased when his telephone rang and delighted with what he heard. The lab had produced a less than perfect but useable set of fingerprints from the victim's burnt hands. He had not allowed himself to hope for these and celebrated by collecting them himself and taking them to be checked with records.

Momentarily, he contemplated recalling Hunter from his telephoning, but decided that evidence from Harlow, even if completely negative, was needed to justify the invasion of the Carr household on a search for something as damning and frightening, in the general public's view, as fingerprints. He felt quite convinced himself that the body in the lab was Gary Carr's and he itched to pursue what he was sure would be a definite identification. He made a pact with himself. He would devote the next three-quarters of an hour to single-minded study of the reports of the series of break-ins at a number of DIY stores during the last few weeks, and then take Hannah out for lunch. He made a brief call to arrange to pick her up, then reseated himself resolutely in front of a large red file to earn his treat.

An hour later he was chauffeuring his wife along the dusty main road that led up the valley to Crossley Bridge, a couple of miles out of Cloughton, where his favourite pub, the Tiller and Tipple, straddled the canal. He parked the car and walked down Old Cawsey, a cobbled ginnel that led down to the water. The sun had dried and blackened the moss between the stones underfoot and now it glinted on the aluminium alloy of the barrels stacked by the entrance. The pub was a converted warehouse standing right on the bank with loading doors on each floor which had puzzled Browne as a child by opening on to nothing. He had used to imagine the occupants of the building absent-mindedly setting off to take a walk and falling from the doors, to take instead an unexpected swim below. Ivy grew up the wall now and was fast engulfing the sign which had once swung over the door.

Two barges were moored on the canal, returned and waiting to accommodate the next parties of holiday-makers. Behind them, on the opposite bank, a warehouse had been converted to offices for a boat hire firm. Its surface had been cleaned and its window frames painted a sparkling white. Browne preferred the blackened stone of the pub which was less obtrusive against the water and surrounding greenery. Gas canisters for use in the boats, painted in vivid reds and blues, were locked in a huge wire cage under the bottom row of office windows. The cobbles above the towpath had been covered with a paved garden.

There was just sufficient movement in the air to fracture the images of the boats in the water. On the far side of the canal the ground rose abruptly. A shopping street ran beneath the slope and Browne noticed that both a greengrocer and a second-hand book dealer had caused an obstruction by spreading their wares on the pavement. Above the main street, several anonymous tower blocks jostled with terraces of small houses, the privacy of their backyards jealously guarded. Further up still, a scrubby, worn-looking hillside, in shadow, stretched up to a horizon punctuated with pylons, telegraph wires and stunted trees which sulked at the buffeting of a wind which had relented in the face of the heat wave but not long enough for the trees to recover and flourish.

Hannah sat at a rough plank table in the yard and Browne investigated the dim interior of the pub. When his eyes had adjusted, he found the bar really was still almost empty. In a fit of pleased extravagance he ordered Hannah's favourite smoked

49

salmon sandwiches with their salad and placed her plate and glass smugly in front of her. She thanked him by giving him the benefit of her frank opinion of his treatment of his daughter. Unmoved, he watched her mobile features scold him as vigorously as her carefully tabulated arguments. Knowing she was right and that, shortly, he was going to capitulate, he stopped listening and instead admired the even white teeth that Virginia had inherited as they attacked the brown bread. Hannah enjoyed food as much as he did himself. In fact, she enjoyed everything, facing whatever chanced with a wide freckled grin and a challenging grey glance.

Having paused for breath, she renewed her attack. 'It won't do, Tom, to demand a mature responsibility in her dealings with other people, but to expect, when she's dealing with you, that she'll obey your wishes to the letter as she very properly did when she was five.'

Browne hoped that the inspector from Crossley Bridge sub-station, whom he had recognised two tables away, was not within earshot. 'I suppose you've got a point,' he admitted. 'In fact, I'm thinking of telling her to take a year out to get herself sorted. Twelve months in a dead-end job will make her see . . .'

Hannah shook her head and her shoulder-length brown hair fell back from her eyes. 'Correction. She will think of taking a year out and having her place held over till next year. She'll suggest it this evening and you'll agree – reluctantly.'

'Your round,' was Browne's ambiguous reply.

Chapter 5

By eleven o'clock the next morning, Browne's patience and industry were rewarded by a temporarily almost empty in-tray and a call from an Inspector Buckley of Essex County Constabulary. His men had trailed round every garage in the Yellow Pages that came within their compass. They had gone beyond the terms of the request and checked the cheap hotels and boarding houses for a man of the right type who had arrived at the relevant time. They had come up with nothing.

'Do you want us to keep trying?' Buckley offered, affably.

Browne thought not. He had the wherewithal to find out one way or the other about Gary Carr, and he thought he now had sufficient grounds to use it. He declined politely, thanked the inspector punctiliously and rang off.

Hunter came in as the receiver was replaced. 'That was Harlow,' Browne informed him. 'No word of your friend.'

Hunter frowned. 'He certainly isn't that. I've been thinking, sir. Couldn't we put out an appeal for him on television and in the papers?'

Browne was halfway into his coat. 'We can if we have to, Jerry, but I think we've enough on Carr to bring out those dabs now. Can you get on to Donaldson about it and send him round after me? I fancy being there myself when Theresa Carr's put on the spot.'

Sorry not to be invited along, Hunter trudged off to contact the fingerprint expert. His mild disappointment turned to fierce resentment when, through the window, he observed Mitchell, his tail decidedly up, climbing into the driving seat of Browne's car.

The lady about to be confronted was engaged in another interview. She wanted to help and reassure her visitor almost as much as she

51

wanted to get rid of him. His ineffectual earnestness irritated her. He never seemed to get himself together. In some ways he was like Gary, but he was never guilty of Gary's childish spite. Alan's immaturity took the form of assuming that God would mend the mess he kept making of his life as, in his infancy, his father had mended the toys he kept breaking.

'I don't know how to convince you, Alan. I just know that I'm right.' She pushed the hair off her damp forehead. 'Gary won't do anything. He never has done, except issue tight-lipped threats until he's got over whatever's upset him.'

'I just wish you hadn't mentioned my problem.'

She sighed at his needing to refer, in this coy manner, to his sexual idiosyncrasy. If he couldn't face it himself, with someone who understood and liked him, he could hardly expect the rest of the world to accept it. And she did like him very much most of the time. She tried again. 'Look, you and I spent several evenings together, collecting and checking props for a pageant. Gary knew that it was perfectly innocent, but he was offended because he's always thought marrying me meant monopolising my interest and attention. He's one of those inadequate people who feel threatened whenever they aren't being exclusively considered. It makes him seem arrogant but really his self-image is very weak. He's always expressed his self-dislike as irritation with people he's familiar with and dares to ill-use. He went on at me about spending more time with you than at home with him, at a time when I was too tired to coax him into a more reasonable frame of mind. I answered what he was saying and not what he really meant. I told him that you were perfectly happy with Charles and that accusing me of being up to no good with someone who was gay was about the stupidest criticism he had ever made of me.'

She realised, with horror, that she too was employing euphemisms. 'Up to no good', indeed! And 'gay' was worse. She buried her face in her hands. 'Just believe me. I knew him and he had no intention of ruining your reputation at church or anywhere else, whatever he might have said to you.'

It was untypical of her to show distress by physical mannerisms, and he answered with compunction, putting his limp hand clumsily on her shoulder. 'Theresa, I'm sorry. I shouldn't have come and I'd better go. I'm sure you're right and Gary will have forgotten all about it when he comes home again. You're sure you've recovered from your attack on Sunday? And that I can't do anything for you?'

Repeating her assurances, she pulled herself together long enough to show him out. Then she sat on the bottom stair, chin propped on her hands, and wondered if she could live with her own thoughts for the four hours that had to pass before she could go back to the surgery. Making order out of the frenzied chaos there demanded her utmost concentration and blotted out the madness of the last week. Eight days ago, she had been anticipating the weekend celebration as eagerly as anyone, though the high spot for her was to be not the pageant but the calm dignity of the Festal Evensong with Glyn's music and Zoe's singing. But when Sunday arrived, she hadn't been able to find the strength. She'd missed the special singing at Easter, too, with Gary's mother's last illness. Christmas was the last time she'd heard Zoe sing and that had been before she'd left the choir herself.

She shut her eyes to relive that Christmas Eve midnight service. She had been astonished when Gary had decided to go with her and, from her place in the choir stalls, had craned to see whether anyone would go to sit with him in the far back corner where he spent his occasional visits. The choir had gone up to the Communion rail before the rest of the congregation, so they could sing whilst the vicar communicated everyone else. As they had taken their places behind the screen of the Lady Chapel she had forgotten her worries and given herself up to the music. She remembered the incongruous length of Glyn, perched in front of a toy-sized keyboard with which he gave them their opening chords.

The chapel had been full of rhythmically breathing human flesh. Faces were red against the newly-starched-for-Christmas whiteness of surplices. Tongues and lips were moist and corporeal but the music was unearthly, fusing with the warm darkness, the haloes round the candles and the resinous smell of greenery and creating Christmas. Christmas had been all around her for weeks, in the shops, in the streets, in the surgery, but it was happening here for her now. The euphoria remained as the choir finished the service and descended to the vestry. She had been glad it was Gerald Morgan who had read the final prayer. His voice had the right timbre and hadn't broken the spell. When Gary had come through the vestry door she'd forgotten he was in church. His face had had that haunted, shut down look that she dreaded. She had been enjoying something he couldn't share.

Christine had caught sight of him, summed up the situation and gone over to shake hands. He had returned her 'Happy Christmas', but his eyes had remained dead and when he had turned back to her, the lips had resumed their tight line. 'I'm frozen. Are you ready?' At the beginning he hadn't been like this. She hadn't been quite fair to him with Alan.

Anne-Marie, trying desperately to retrieve the situation, had given him a mock punch. She had played into his hands. His eyes had blazed with a blue-cold fury, and he had doubled up as though the blow had carried the weight of a serious intention. Theresa had wondered whether his frightening pallor had been due to genuine cold or ill-temper, and then she had quickly bundled her daughter out of the room. Gary had followed them outside, a silent, inevitable presence. 'I'm leaving St Oswald's.' She had known, from experience of his moods, that this was not a statement of intent but the first pathetic blow in another trivial cold war. She had been surprised to find that she was not afraid this time. The opening shot hadn't harmed her.

'You've more or less left already.' It had been safer than the retort she'd bitten back, 'Who'd notice?'

As they walked down the road, Anne-Marie had tried to begin a brightly nervous discussion – on phantom pregnancies, of all things, and she had wanted to weep for the strange little girl whose insecure upbringing had brought her to this. The child had confirmed her anxiety by her celerity in retiring to bed.

Theresa had made coffee, returning with steaming mugs to find Gary hunched before the hissing gas fire. She had received physical comfort from sipping the scalding liquid but a paralysing despair had swept over her. Ignoring the mug she had placed in front of him, Gary had lain back in the chair, eyes closed, jaw hanging slack. It could have been a handsome face, framed in springing black hair, with well-shaped brows and lean sallow cheeks, but the jaw was too narrow, expressing his permanent aggrieved irresolution.

She wondered what could be read from her own face. Why had she been afraid of a man of so little account, so self-absorbed? She supposed the self-absorption was frightening, and the fact that she had put her future and that of her children into his

54

hands. She started at the shrilling of the telephone and walked, stiff-limbed, towards it, wondering how long she had sat, gazing unseeing down the hall. Browne's voice brought a momentary panic but she preferred even his interference in her affairs to her own meditations. Maybe she could carry it off and everything would work out. But, whether it did or not, she hadn't really any choice now. She couldn't feel she'd done wrong.

Now he had a body with a name, Browne could get on with his case, find out something of what his victim had been like and why anyone should want him dead. He was so engrossed in planning the afternoon for himself and his team, it took Hunter's return from a late lunch to remind him that he'd missed his own. He filled Hunter in on his interview with Theresa Carr, whilst he munched hastily ordered and less than delectable cheese sandwiches. 'Donaldson found dabs all over the house that matched with the ones we got from the lab. Mrs Carr sat like a block of wood when he told her and the boy behaved almost as strangely. I got a funny feeling, though, not that she didn't care but that she was incapable of expressing grief. And the boy was frightened. The girl made up for them though. Hysterical weeping, self-reproaches that she hadn't tried harder to please him – all the sort of things I'd have expected from the mother. They're a rum lot.' Hunter stared through the window and made the briefest of comments.

Well aware of the reason for his apparent lack of interest, Browne decided to spring the trap. 'Mitchell is anxious we shouldn't assume that this is just a simple domestic. You're the only one who knows anything about the family. What do you think?'

Hunter turned from the window, fetched an upright chair from the door and sat astride it facing the backrest. 'I agree with him,' he announced when he had settled himself. 'Theresa's not simple and the case won't be. But that's not the same as saying I don't think she did it.'

Browne grimaced as he swallowed the last dregs of his cold coffee. 'We're all agreed, then. She won't change her story of the Tuesday night phone call from someone who called himself only Dave. The saga of her mother and the hospital can easily be checked. We can't take it for granted that Carr didn't set off for Harlow even though he doesn't seem to have arrived there.

55

We need to know where he went, if anywhere, after his wife left the house on Tuesday evening. I'm keeping you right out of it at the moment, Jerry. I, with Mitchell as my minion, press everyone hard. You, as their friend, listen to all their little confidences as they try to pump you about what we're thinking.'

Mollified, Hunter nodded. 'How hard have you pressed Theresa?'

Browne scowled. 'Not hard enough to shake her.'

She'd treated him rather like one of the patients she dealt with daily, who considered his symptoms more serious than they were, and who had to be simultaneously reassured and prevented from being a nuisance. She'd told him the call from Harlow had come at about eight o'clock and she'd rung the pub where she'd expected Gary to be at about five past. No one else was in. Frank had been watching a video next door at the Morgans' house and Anne-Marie was at a Confirmation class at the vicarage. Gary had been enthusiastic about both the job and seeing his friend again. He'd come home and rung the number she'd been given.

'Can you remember it?' Browne had asked.

She'd shaken her cool blonde head. 'Only the code. I think that was 0279.'

He had pressed her. 'Isn't that what makes you good at your job – being able to hold details in your head?'

Her manner was detached. 'I'm glad you've been told I'm good at it. And you're right, I do need to have a good memory. But I didn't need to remember this. I wrote it on the pad beside the phone and left it for Gary to refer to. He must have torn it off because it wasn't there when I looked for it after Constable Mitchell had been to see me at the surgery.'

Browne had tried to convince himself that this patiently reasoning creature was a widow whose husband's half-burned body had been identified for certain less than an hour ago. Yet he didn't feel the woman before him was unmoved. The smooth pale exterior showed nothing of her thoughts and feelings and that calm mask could be hiding suffering just as well as guilt or satisfaction.

It occurred to him that, if Hannah died, he might cope in very much the same way. No one else could ever understand their unique and complicated relationship and to give an outsider a partial glimpse of what he'd lost would be an insult, an injury to her. He'd returned to the attack.

56

'How did the caller introduce himself to you?'

'Just "Dave from Harlow".'

'And then what?'

'He explained his predicament.' Browne had let the ensuing silence continue until she had to go on. 'One of his garage hands had had both legs broken in a road accident. He was halfway through a cylinder head job on an old Peugeot diesel and apparently he and Gary had worked together on one years ago so he thought of him.'

'I presume,' Browne had cut in, 'that they'd been out of touch for some time or you'd have known something about him.' She'd nodded at that. 'So how did he know your phone number?'

She'd replied immediately and calmly, 'I can't help you there, I'm afraid,' but her fingers were pleating the pastel checks of her cotton skirt. She'd helped her husband pack clothes and tools, intending to drive him to the station but, when her mother had phoned, she'd left him to finish alone and told him to get a taxi.

'Good for her,' Hunter had put in. 'It's her car.'

Browne continued. 'Luckily they hadn't loaded his belongings into the car boot. She left straight after the call at nine fifteen and didn't return until getting on for eleven.'

Hunter nodded. 'That figures. When the old lady shouts, Theresa runs. Not that Mrs Kelly ever does anything so unladylike as shouting.'

'You know the mother too?'

Hunter shrugged. 'Slightly. More by reputation than personal acquaintance. Whatever was wrong with her, she probably deserved it.'

'Mrs Carr didn't seem sure. The hospitalisation was for tests as much as treatment, though she says the old lady has had some heart trouble. It shouldn't have been more than two or three minutes' drive, but it took ten because the car was playing up. When she'd coaxed it into the car park at the sheltered housing complex, she rang her son at the Morgans' house to come and look at it.'

'Mrs Kelly can't have been desperately ill then,' Hunter commented. He swung his leg over the chair back and wandered to the window.

Browne looked to see how much carpet pile was left on Hunter's habitual route. 'Apparently she deteriorated alarmingly towards ten o'clock when Mrs Carr rang for the doctor, Fenwick. She works for him and Mrs Kelly is his patient. Fenwick sent her to the Infirmary and Mrs Carr went with her in the ambulance. Frank followed in the car and waited to drive his mother back.'

Hunter prowled again, pondering. 'What about Anne-Marie?' he asked presently.

'When Mrs Carr realised she wouldn't get home until late she rang the vicarage and left a message for Anne-Marie to be taken to the Morgans' house. Frank picked her up from there when he returned the car. The Morgans had lent him theirs so that he could bring his mother home if he couldn't repair the fault in hers.' Browne got up and opened the window wider. 'I need some strong tea and ten minutes away from all this.'

Rather more than ten minutes were enjoyed in the canteen but when, at four o'clock, he summoned his team Browne felt clear-headed again. As he waited for them he collected the potted plants variously disposed about his office and placed them on a battered grey filing cabinet by the window. Each morning his cleaner arranged them artistically on the surfaces of her choice and later in the day Browne, who was no horticulturist but who had not the heart to let them die, collected them together to make watering quick and easy. Satisfied that they would survive another twenty-four hours in the stuffy room, he appropriated the only comfortable armchair. This piece of furniture looked particularly out of place on the worn carpet in company with several more functional wooden seats and a scratched and stained desk that bore tell-tale white rings from the base of Browne's frequently filled coffee mug.

The only other island of civilisation was his bookcase of well-polished oak which contained a wide selection of detective fiction, beginning with Dickens and *The Mystery of Edwin Drood*. He had moved it in a short time ago after discovering that Hunter too found their fictional counterparts entertaining. He was amused that his other colleagues offered no comment and made a point of not borrowing them.

Dean was last to arrive and condemned to an uncomfortable stool as they considered the facts so far at their disposal. Carr had been a skilled labourer, often out of work. His wife's job had kept the family. He'd been shiftless and despised but not, as far as they knew, vicious or depraved. Who'd want him dead?

'His wife?' Bellamy offered, sliding into the chair Hunter had just vacated as he set off on his first tour of the office this session.

'She's got to be the first person we consider,' Browne agreed, 'but we can't concentrate on her exclusively. There's a lot I want to know about a lot of people. If Mrs Carr wanted to be rid of her husband, she's independent. She'd only got to throw him out and divorce him when they'd been apart long enough.'

'She's RC,' put in Hunter from the window.

Browne swivelled his chair to face Hunter indignantly. 'You said she was a pillar of St Oswald's!'

Hunter nodded. 'Yes, she's that as well. Gary Carr was nothing in particular. Monica Kelly's a Catholic and was furious that Theresa became non-practising when she married. Theresa's never been quite happy about it. The vicar knows more about it than I do.'

'Then that's one more thing I intend to ask him.'

Bellamy returned to his original suggestion. 'What sort of woman is Mrs Carr, physically?'

Mitchell considered himself the more discriminating judge. 'Blonde, good figure, interesting face. Easy on the eye though not beautiful.' He paused for breath.

Bellamy grinned and shook his head. 'I meant, is she strong enough to have lugged her husband to the spinney by herself? Perhaps she had help? Maybe a boyfriend.'

Dean became infected with the idea. 'Perhaps she used to meet him in the spinney. Perhaps they killed him there.'

Browne shook his head. 'Shouldn't think so. If they did they didn't leave him there. Too many people went there between Tuesday and Sunday.'

Hunter turned from the window. 'I want to know where the body was kept until Saturday night. It must have been more than a bit high by then. If Theresa had it she could hardly have dumped it in the cellar and just hoped the youngsters wouldn't go down.'

Browne opened his top drawer and removed a pile of action sheets, neatly filled in. 'We want to know as much as possible from anyone who knew Carr in any capacity. I don't want his

wife interviewed again until we know a good deal more about her.'
He handed a sheet to Dean. 'You and Bellamy go and chat to all
the neighbours who are in a position to watch the Carrs' comings
and goings. Find out in particular whether anyone saw Gary Carr
leave on Tuesday night and whether they have any suspicions that
Theresa might have a man friend tucked away somewhere. Go into
the pub on the corner and if Carr didn't drink there, find out where
he did. Get started now before the husbands come home and tell
their wives to mind what they're saying. Oh, and miss out the
Morgans. I want to see them myself.'

He picked up another sheet. 'Mitchell, you can see the two
youngsters when they get in at tea time. Take Jennie Smith with
you and let Mrs Carr be present if she wants to be. Same questions
but much more tactfully phrased. Add any you're bright enough to
think up for yourselves. I trust your discretion except when you're
bickering with colleagues.'

Finally, he turned to Hunter. 'You're in an equivocal position,
Jerry, since all these folk are your friends. If you know where
Carr did some of this casual work we keep hearing about you
could nose about in that direction.'

Hunter nodded. 'It was often in that garage in Archer Road
where Frank has his Saturday job. And, talking of young Frank,
sir, I keep remembering how he offered up that dolly catch on
Sunday afternoon and the look on his face when he set off after
Zoe. I'm pretty sure he knew what she was going to find under
that tree.'

Chapter 6

On Wednesdays, Christopher Fenwick held no evening surgery and so Theresa Carr was free to attend Compline at four o'clock. She loved the simple old service and was devoutly thankful that the ecclesiastical powers had not seen fit to supersede it with an up-to-date version in the Alternative Service Book. The other attenders had gone, all nine of them, and the vicar had retired into his own vestry. She was alone in church.

She had read somewhere that you were only ever essentially yourself when alone, but she wasn't sure about it. When she was alone, she found she suffered from a strange embarrassment, as though she couldn't stop acting the rôle she showed to the world, and yet she could see the foolishness of trying to deceive herself or trying to pretend before God. Did she believe in God? She wasn't sure any more. She'd been through a lifetime of religious experience – at least, she thought she had. Now she felt, most of the time, that He wasn't there.

She remembered an occasion when she was sixteen, sitting in her bedroom at her mother's house, poring over her New Testament and demanding to feel the undeniable presence of God. She remembered vividly the answering warm glow she had felt and enjoyed and then, immediately, doubted. It was an illusion. She'd felt it because she'd expected to feel it. How would she recognise God's love and approval anyway? God was like her mother. She had to do and be exactly what He wanted, give up her own identity. She'd read about people who'd been converted, given up their self-seeking lives in obedience to God. She had only tried to transfer her allegiance from her mother to Him. She hadn't been able to make a great renunciation for His sake. She had never belonged to herself, been her own to give, either to God or to Gary.

She should never have married him. He'd needed someone who thought he was wonderful. Why hadn't he married a pretty little fool? She'd been too quick-tongued for him. She'd finished his sentences for him, not with what he was going to say but with what he really meant. Often he didn't even know he meant it. She'd destroyed his fragile self-confidence and despised him because he'd let her. By staying with him she'd destroyed them both. Yet she had a dreadful feeling, now that it was too late, that she could have broken from her mother's thralldom, that she could have loved Gary, that the respect and affection she now received from her friends and colleagues could have built her self-esteem so that she didn't need to violate his. If only she could go back just a couple of weeks. But there was nothing she could do about it now.

She became aware that she was no longer alone, although she hadn't raised her head or opened her eyes. Only when she did so did Philip Garside step forward and place his hand on her shoulder. 'I'd been planning to invite you to tea,' he told her, 'hoping you could tell us some way in which we might help you, but I'm afraid there's a policeman waiting in the vicarage. There isn't much I can tell him but I'll have to do what I can. I'll call round later if I may.'

Still kneeling, she nodded, her expression blank. Then she scrambled to her feet and made her way outside, genuflecting as she reached the aisle before turning towards the west door. Philip Garside crossed the church garden to the vicarage and thence to his study. There he met his wife who was placing a tea tray on his desk. She withdrew, closing the door behind her.

Seated in his visitors' chair, Browne watched the vicar as he chose to settle himself behind his desk. So, he was on the side of his church members against the police. He reminded Browne of photographs of his father and uncles, gathered on family occasions. There was something old-fashioned about the pin-striped, double-breasted suit and thick, brown, slightly waving hair, brushed off his face and to the side, not Brylcreemed as his father's had been, but lying as neat and flat as if it were. Either this or his office lent him a maturity beyond his probable thirty years. The room was a fitting background for him, book-lined, white-painted and respectable.

Garside indicated the tea tray and quickly disposed of his duties as a host. 'Help yourself to tea and whatever else Jane has served us. How can I help you, Chief Inspector?'

Appreciating equally his straightforward approach and the chance to pour tea exactly as he liked it, Browne helped himself and made his reply. 'By telling me, if you will, as much as possible about your parish and the people in it.' He retired back to his chair with a brimming cup and a plate of buttered scone.

'Beginning with?'

'With Alan Priestley, for the sake of starting somewhere. He discovered the body, did nothing about it except plant a religious tract beside it, then turned up on your doorstep, quoting wildly from the Psalms, apparently hoping you'd soothe his conscience by telling him he'd done the right thing. Would you say he was slightly deranged?'

Garside shook his head without any hesitation, but then paused, wondering how to explain. 'If he were clinically certifiable, I wouldn't allow him the freedom of the pulpit. He has certain eccentric views which some of the congregation condemn as superstition and others find amusing, but I don't agree with every public statement of my other lay reader either, and I'm sure my own theology is not always approved of. You'll have to enquire elsewhere about that.'

Browne nodded and chewed appreciatively. 'What's a lay reader?'

Reaching into a drawer, the vicar drew out a leaflet and pushed it across the desk top. 'Read it for yourself but, briefly, it's a man or woman with a secular job, who works alongside an ordained minister, usually within a parish. The work is voluntary. Here, it mostly consists of reading lessons and prayers, preaching and visiting the old and the sick.'

Browne pocketed the leaflet and put his empty cup down hopefully. 'Could you give me some concrete examples of Priestley's eccentricities, besides the ones I've observed? What's his secular job, by the way?'

The vicar's gesture invited Browne to replenish his cup and plate. 'He's a supply teacher, covering for regular teachers who're ill or on courses. Eccentricities? He interprets Scripture much more literally than people at St Oswald's like. For example, he has what he calls a promise box, obtained from some society whose views he shares, filled with 365 texts for a year. Each morning he takes one out, accepting it as God's personal message to himself for that day. And why shouldn't he? He thinks clerical robing is superstitious. He's especially disapproving of choir robes.'

Suddenly, he grinned and his face lost its rather ponderous quality. 'If he came into the vestry as I do, when the boy choristers are arriving, and read the unseemly library of tee-shirts that the cassocks and surplices expediently cover, he might change his mind. Though I'm afraid the words on their chests more accurately indicate the direction of their thoughts than the ones on their lips.'

'So he's just a bit naïve?'

Garside considered. 'I suppose you could put it like that. He seems muddled and misguided to people who like to have their theology or philosophy systematised or more theoretical than practical, but that doesn't mean he's been deprived of his fair share of snippets of the truth. He has a right to preach them and we can learn from him.'

'And what about his opposite number?'

'He has his hands full shooting down Alan's literalism. He makes free use of the names of all the modern theologians but I doubt whether he's made a careful study of what they propose. He's very firm on what he doesn't believe. Alan thinks lighted candles are anathema and Gerald panics if they aren't lit as though they are necessary to activate the Almighty's hearing aid. The Alternative Service Book is a positive armoury for them to do battle with.'

Browne was puzzled by the vicar's obvious satisfaction with the situation. 'Is this constant battle what you want?'

Garside shrugged. 'If it exists I want the congregation to see that it does. We can't help ourselves discover the ultimate truth by presenting a false front. This congregation has to make its own decisions, based on its own meditations. I make full use of every method this church offers me, to encourage people to work out their own relationship with God, including its personnel.' He grinned again. 'Besides, I'd be denying myself a great deal of entertainment if I only allowed the readers to function where their views overlapped with mine. I don't sit tutting when I disagree with them either. I like my faith to include mystery. It's a perfectly natural condition. It seems to me that those people who can't accept it either live in a state of perpetual anxiety or protect themselves by deliberately wearing blinkers of one kind or another.'

Throughout the conversation, a small tabby cat, perched on an upright chair, had dabbed and jabbed at the large tortoiseshell on the floor below. Suddenly tiring of this irritation, the tortoiseshell made off, whereupon the tabby took a flying leap in pursuit. With surprising agility for a beast whose stomach almost trailed the ground, the tortoiseshell rolled over and delivered a fierce body blow that deprived the tabby of breath. Immediately, as though in apology, she began to lick the tabby and the whole procedure ended with reciprocated washing, each obligingly dealing with the other's most inaccessible parts.

Browne, who liked cats, smiled. 'An object lesson if we needed one. Do your lay readers end their spats with such friendly cooperation?'

Garside scooped up the tabby. 'They do quite often. Meet the vicarage cats, Mag and Nunc.' He dropped the one he held into a basket by the desk where the other joined her.

'Tell me about the Carr family,' Browne invited. 'Gary Carr first.' He noticed that Garside's consternation at the change of subject was allayed.

'I didn't like him,' the vicar admitted frankly. 'He was the sort who'd come to a pie and pea supper and want to know what he could have because he didn't like pies and he wasn't keen on peas. He belonged to that fringe group of attenders who came often enough to feel that the church ought to do something for him but not sufficiently often for him to feel obliged to offer anything in return. He never became a familiar enough figure for the congregation to feel they could stop making much of him to encourage him along. Where he is now, he's probably trying alternate attendances at heaven and hell, hoping they'll both make a fuss of him to gain his permanent membership.'

Browne felt faintly shocked. This was a somewhat unusual clergyman. He waited, knowing Garside would continue. 'Coming to and then leaving church was one of his favourite weapons against Theresa.'

'I understand she's a Catholic.'

The vicar nodded. 'Her parents were and she remained in communion with the RCs until her first pregnancy. Then she began to imagine what life would be like with seventeen children and an out-of-work husband. She defected to us and birth control. It cost her a lot and she still feels guilty. She's untiring in her work

65

here as though being a first-class Anglican is part of her penance. She gave the children aggressively Catholic names. Francis Xavier and Anne-Marie Bernadette raised a few eyebrows at St Oswald's, I imagine.'

'And what do you think about it?'

Philip Garside smiled. 'I'm not the sort of Anglican who thinks he'll sit inside the gates of heaven, waving to the Catholics outside. I'm glad to have her as a church member and a friend. She hasn't had much of a life really. She's made a grand job of rearing those two youngsters, considering everything. They're a great comfort to her now although she worries over them too.'

Browne remembered what Hunter had said. 'From what I've heard of her, I'm surprised the mother allowed such a match. Does she attend your church too?'

'No, I told you, she's still a Catholic, though I sometimes visit her for Theresa's sake.' He cast his eyes upwards. 'It doesn't do either of us any good. All old ladies grumble, some cheerfully, some less so. Monica's grumbles are always manipulative. She isn't relieving her feelings so much as making you feel obliged to do or say whatever she's decided you should. I find it difficult not to be managed by her. Theresa, who was trained from babyhood to be an extension of her mother, finds it almost impossible to stand up to her. I think marrying Gary was Theresa's one desperate act of rebellion. She did it quickly, without thinking about it too long or she'd have lost the impetus and the courage.'

Mag and Nunc had left their shared basket and whichever was the tabby was scratching at the door. Garside rose to let her out as Browne asked, 'Why do the children worry Mrs Carr?'

As the tabby departed, the tortoiseshell repossessed herself of the basket, using all the space to stretch sensually before curling up and composing herself for further sleep. Garside poked her with his foot. 'That's the sum total of her exercise for the day. I ought to throw her out but I haven't the heart. She doesn't like outside.'

Instead of retreating again behind his desk, he took the armchair opposite Browne, as though he had decided it was worth appealing to him on Theresa's behalf. 'She thinks because she's been very unhappy that they must have been too.'

'And were they?'

Garside shrugged. 'Frank wasn't – isn't. He's a perfectly normal, bright seventeen-year-old, likely to do well in his A levels and then at university.'

'And the girl?'

There was a pause which answered Browne before he received his reply. 'She's a strange child, turned fifteen but in most respects still a little girl. She does very well at school too but Theresa's concerned because she's never rebelled or identified with her own generation. She strikes me as unnaturally docile and, of course, that makes her the apple of her grandmother's eye. Gary was often very irritable with her. She told her mother that her father hated her and Theresa sometimes felt that was what the child really believed.'

Realising that Garside would tell him nothing that might incriminate any of the living members of the Carr family, Browne tried an abrupt change of subject. 'Sergeant Hunter has told me, reluctantly, that Mr Priestley is reported to have homosexual tendencies. Is it true? And if so, why didn't you mention it? Wouldn't you call that an eccentricity?'

Garside returned his challenging glare. 'Before you left, I would equally reluctantly have told you, not that I think it could have any bearing on Gary Carr's death.' His expression changed as he finished speaking but he kept the idea which had obviously just occurred to him to himself.

'That's for me to decide,' Browne told him, sternly. 'Please don't edit your information.'

The lecture was cut short by the shrilling of the telephone. Garside excused himself, reached for it and let it quack into his ear. It was obviously bad news. The vicar offered his caller a few words of reassurance which failed to soothe as the quacking became hysterical. He looked up at Browne. 'One of your minions has arrested this lady's husband. Could you continue your questions after I've calmed her down and stopped her doing something stupid?'

Browne rose and gathered his belongings. 'Certainly, if you tell me as we go exactly what you were doing last Tuesday evening from half-past seven.'

The vicar's face registered first astonishment, then indignation before he grinned and obliged. Then he drove away and Browne paused to rest his notebook on the garden wall. He recorded the time of the Confirmation class and Garside's affirmation that

Anne-Marie had remained with him until he dropped her at the gate of the Morgans' house. He had been glad of the telephone call that had interrupted his interview. Information always came to him filtered through the prejudices and personalities of those who offered it. He wanted some time to weigh up this vicar before deciding what to make of what he had to say.

Chapter 7

DC Mitchell walked for the second time up Burnley Brow, speculating wistfully about the small square rooms the houses would contain, with comfortable central heating and low ceilings, easy to reach when decorating. The windows of the bungalows could be cleaned without ladders and the well laid out small plots around them looked easy to maintain. He felt no envy though. Suddenly he realised he was seeing the estate through his parents' eyes. It was just what they needed at their time of life but he could not imagine living here himself. Still less could he see Virginia here. She'd fit in better on the sturdily built Heath Lees estate where he'd been reared, rough and ready though it was.

His observations left him less time than usual to appreciate the charms of Constable Smith, but perhaps it was as well, as any particular notice he took of her now would be reported back to Ginny in short order. She had already rung the bell and he could see somebody approaching through the frosted glass panel in the brightly painted but flimsy looking door. Theresa Carr opened it, cool in a sleeveless cotton dress, the pale hair tied at the nape of her neck with a matching scarf. Mitchell remembered his description of her to Bellamy and decided he'd omitted to mention a grace and a kind of – perhaps refinement was the word. They followed her up the minute hall and into a small square sitting room, overlooking a scant forty square yards of garden and a low wall.

Anne-Marie stopped writing in her diary and deliberately caught Mitchell's eye before pretending to ignore him and moving over to the sideboard to put the pen and book into a drawer. She recrossed the room to her seat, taking tiny steps and glancing out of the corner of her eye to make sure she still had his attention. Then she sat demurely, ankles crossed, hands in her lap, looking down.

Jennie decided that here was just such a minx as Zoe, though her methods were different. She grinned to herself. Flat-chested, bashful maidens were not much to Mitchell's taste.

Mrs Carr waved them to a pastel-coloured Dralon sofa and pulled up a low table in front of them. 'I'm quite happy for you to talk to the youngsters but Frank's been helping old Mr Medway in his garden this afternoon. I volunteered him. All of us will find the next few days easier to get through if we've plenty to do, especially if it's to help someone else. If he isn't back in a few minutes I'll telephone for him. He knows you're coming. Perhaps you'll have a cup of tea. Annie's put the kettle on.' She settled herself in an armchair that matched the sofa whilst Anne-Marie walked daintily in front of Mitchell and out to the kitchen.

Jennie smiled. 'It's nice to have a grown-up daughter to share the chores.'

Watching Theresa Carr respond, Mitchell was glad to have Jennie with him. He was feeling intimidated by both the silly child and the withdrawn yet self-possessed mother. 'They're both quite sensible and easy to live with,' she was saying, 'but Frank, at least, hasn't always been. When he was eleven, I couldn't decide whether to throw him into the canal or to jump in myself. He was so naughty at home I never knew what he'd do next. He hated school and played truant sometimes.'

'Sounds pretty normal to me,' Mitchell put in.

'I suppose so.' She tucked her feet under her on the chair. 'He was different from other small boys though. He'd leave his toys and spend all morning lying in the drive, watching the scurryings of a colony of ants. He did far from brilliantly at school before he went into the sixth form but when he was much smaller he'd watch Open University science lectures on television and seemed to enjoy them. I used to try to read stories to him but he'd wriggle off my knee and ask things like "How does the piano work?" or "What's inside my head?" I jibbed at the latter but we took the front away and investigated inside the piano. He's very musical but he resisted all attempts to make him learn the piano and the violin. Then, when the pressure was off him, he saved up enough money of his own to buy a second-hand guitar and practised assiduously. It was always restless, exciting rock music. He found it very satisfying and he's teaching me to understand it. I didn't bring him up, really. He raised himself.'

70

Mitchell was taken aback. They hadn't asked anything yet, and from her appearance he hadn't judged her to be a woman who talked for the sake of it. She went on speaking quickly, anxious to fill up the silence and keep the initiative from them. 'His friends were often lame dogs. He'd tell me their troubles and bring them home sometimes. He liked his own company, though. Until recently he spent hours in his own room. I think he found the family boring.'

She broke off with obvious relief as her daughter, protected by a flowered and frilly apron, pushed a tea trolley into the room. Anne-Marie poured tea and milk and distributed pretty china plates. Then she sat down and awaited her questioning.

She readily described her activities on the Tuesday evening of her father's departure. She had set off to walk to her Confirmation class and waved to the family when she reached the gate. 'That was the last time I saw my father,' was uttered solemnly. She had found the class very interesting. Mr Garside's talks to the young people were always very interesting. He had kindly given her a lift back to Auntie Christine's. No, he hadn't waited until he had seen her enter the house. Her friends, Paula and Helen, were in the back of the car and he'd driven off to deliver them.

No, she hadn't been surprised that Mummy had been to Granny's flat. Mummy often had to visit Granny. It was her duty because Granny was getting elderly. Anne-Marie did her best to help out too, and it was easier now that Granny had moved into the sheltered housing because of her angina. No, it wasn't very bad usually. It was funny, it always seemed to get bad when Mummy was specially busy with something else, but she helped all she could and so did Frank quite often.

Yes, she'd been quite surprised that Daddy had gone to Harlow to work. When Mr Garside had said he wasn't in, she'd thought he'd just gone for a drink. She couldn't remember if he'd ever talked about a friend called David, but he'd sometimes talked about 'the lads' he used to work with. He was probably one of them. Yes, she'd had a lot to do for the patronal festival. She wasn't in the choir so she'd stayed at home on Friday evening and watched television. She hadn't got a very good voice but she sang with the Sunday School children on Sunday morning. She'd been St Oswald's page in the pageant. There'd been a lot to learn. She was very sorry Daddy hadn't been able to see it. Once he'd

71

even practised the lines with her. It had all gone off very well though.

Mitchell watched the girl carefully, ready to stop his questions if she showed signs of too much distress, but throughout the interview she stared at him solemnly as a months-old baby does, without wavering and without apparent self-consciousness, observing him, chiefly, he felt, to see how he was reacting to her.

'When it was over,' she went on, 'I was very tired, but I stayed up and made coffee for Auntie Christine and Zoe. I went to bed as soon as they left and Mummy brought me some drinking chocolate up to my room for a treat. And Frank didn't call me a spoilt brat like he usually does.'

She stopped speaking as an attractive curly-haired youth clattered through the hall and appeared in the sitting-room doorway, looking ruefully at his soiled hands and jeans. 'Sorry to keep you waiting.' He grinned apologetically. Turning to his mother, he added, 'You know what it's like getting away from Mr Medway when he's describing his plans for the garden . . .'

Constable Smith stood up. 'I was parched and that tea was wonderful. How about us women washing up now whilst Constable Mitchell talks to Frank?' She began collecting cups and stacking them on the trolley and, after a momentary hesitation, Anne-Marie helped her whilst Frank sat down opposite Mitchell. Mrs Carr opened the door for them to push the trolley through but didn't follow them out of the room.

Mitchell shot his colleague a glance that said, 'Nice try,' and turned his attention to Frank. Jennie shrugged and set about her self-appointed task with good grace. Anne-Marie having elected to wash, she grabbed a tea cloth and contemplated the girl's back view. She wondered if the little-girl look had been created to avoid responsibility. Did she have to tie her hair back with ribbon and wear such short skirts? She supposed Zoe Morgan did the same but the effect she created was quite different. That was it, of course. Anne-Marie thought that looking as good as Zoe meant copying what Zoe did. She supposed that Anne-Marie couldn't help the gap between her two upper incisors, which, when she smiled, reminded Jennie of little Felicity Hunter who was only seven.

'What's your name?' Anne-Marie demanded, then, obviously not really interested. 'I got an A for my GCSE essay today.'

'It's Jennie. Well done. What was your essay about?'

Having run the hot water, Anne-Marie began transferring the load of crockery from the trolley to the draining board. 'We had to describe three ways in which we'd like to change our lives.'

'That sounds interesting. What did you choose?'

For the first time, Anne-Marie's voice rang with sincerity. 'I said I wished I could look like Zoe. I didn't mention her name of course. She came here yesterday, wearing big dangly earrings and a candy-striped blouse unbuttoned and tied across her bust and the sleeves pushed up above her elbows. She looked great. If I did that I'd just look as if I hadn't had time to get dressed properly.'

Constable Smith began to dry a delicate china dish with great care. 'What suits Zoe wouldn't suit you. You're different types. Why don't you go to a shop with lots of fitting rooms and just keep trying things on until you learn what makes you look good?'

Contemplating this revolutionary idea caused Anne-Marie to knock a cup against the hot tap. She examined it in a panic. 'Thank goodness it isn't chipped, although Daddy can't say much about it now can he? Anyway' – returning to her previous subject – 'Zoe caught her earring in my duvet cover when we were listening to her Shaun Shannon tape and it made her ear bleed.'

Jennie dried another cup. 'What else did you want to change?'

'I said I wanted a really happy home.' She dropped a handful of teaspoons into the cutlery drainer. 'Do you think Zoe's uncle Gerald would like to have me for a daughter? He and Mummy are quite friendly and there's no reason why they shouldn't be now. Or Mr Priestley, maybe. She's quite friendly with him too. Zoe says Mummy couldn't marry him because he's queer. I suppose he is a bit strange. Anyway, Mummy will have to wait a bit. It wouldn't be respectable just yet. Be careful with that teapot won't you?'

Jennie took it and wrapped the tea cloth round it, patting it dry. 'And the third change you'd make?'

But Anne-Marie had lost interest. 'Oh, just to be famous for something. Didn't Frank look a mess when he came in? Gran doesn't like him going to Mr Medway's. She says he's a vulgar old man and she can't imagine why Grandad was so friendly with him. He's always saying a rude word beginning with B. I think it was because of the gardening. He and Grandad used to grow gooseberries. They were always grumbling about b——.

capsid bugs.' She let out an unamused laugh then poured away the hot water. 'Grandad told Mr Medway he could have all his gardening things when he knew he was going to die. Mr Medway didn't need them, he'd got plenty of his own so he just kept them in the garage. Anyway, Granny got them all back a couple of weeks ago. She said there was nothing about it in Grandad's will and they'll be better going to someone who'll make good use of them.' Anne-Marie wandered out of the kitchen. Constable Smith hung the tea cloth to dry and followed her.

Theresa Carr and Mitchell were chatting and Frank had disappeared. 'Anne-Marie's been telling me about her essay on how she'd like to change her life.'

'Has she?' Theresa shrugged. 'Never mind, Annie. You're being very brave coping with school at all. I'm sure your next one will be up to your usual standard.'

Anne-Marie, reseated on her buffet, ankles recrossed, hands refolded, regarded Jennie with a half smile. Mitchell seemed to have a thundercloud just above his head. In a silent exchange of glances, the two constables decided there was no more to be said.

After they left, Theresa reached for a magazine and leafed through it, unseeing. For ten minutes neither she nor her daughter spoke. Then they heard the back door opening.

'There's Frank back again. Could you begin the vegetables for me for supper? There's a good girl.'

Frank stood aside to let his sister pass, then closed the door behind her before coming to stand beside his mother. 'I rode my bike to the chemist's in the precinct, but I'm sure nobody followed me, so I didn't go in. I didn't say anything wrong, did I?'

Theresa buried her face in her hands and spoke through her fingers. 'No, you were very astute. Frank, how are you going to pick up the threads again and do well in your A levels with all this on your mind and your conscience?'

He gave her shoulders an encouraging squeeze. 'It isn't on my conscience. I think, in the circumstances, I did what was right. I can live with it.'

His mother commended herself for suggesting the gardening. An afternoon of physical activity had taken the drawn lines from his face and given him back a little of his normal colour as well as easing his mind.

'Come on,' Frank admonished her, 'we're beginning to use Annie as a servant. Let's give her a hand with the spud bashing.'

Constables Mitchell and Smith walked down the short drive and gained the pavement before voicing their thoughts. Then they spoke simultaneously.

'That girl's either playing stupid games with us or else she's seriously disturbed.'

'What a waste of time. As soon as he'd told me everything we know already she sent him off with a prescription his grandmother had to have before the chemist closed.'

Mitchell grinned. 'Go on, you first.' He listened to Jennie's account of the bizarre conversation she had had with Anne-Marie. He looked thoughtful but made no comment beyond, 'We're always being told to look for deviations from anyone's usual habits. I wonder why Frank didn't call his sister a spoiled brat when she got her cocoa in bed on Saturday night. Mrs Carr didn't seem to mind Anne-Marie prattling to you. Do we gather there's nothing she can tell us we'd be interested in?'

Jennie shrugged. 'I'm interested in the fact that she seems to think her mother's been waiting for the chance to take up with Gerald Morgan – if she really does think that and isn't busy laying red herrings for us. And does she really not know what Zoe means by "queer"? Anyway, how did you get on?'

'Like I said, I got nowhere. Frank told me he watched a video at the Morgans' house last Tuesday, not a horror epic but a wildlife programme Zoe had recorded about ants. Then he drove Glyn Morgan's car to his grandmother's flat, sprayed some WD40 on his mother's plugs, helped his mother minister to his grandmother and drove her back from the hospital to the flat so that they could get both cars back home. On Friday he played his guitar and read a book between tea and nine thirty, then collected Zoe from choir practice and took her and himself for an illegal drink. On Saturday, he went to work in the morning, then did some more work on his mother's car which got him out of the Sunday School concert. He went to a rehearsal, then in the evening played his part in the pageant, snogged in the spinney afterwards and took Zoe home with him in a good enough mood not to tease his sister when she expected waitress service in her room. Maybe Anne-Marie was being tactful and keeping out of the way of the young lovers. He saw nothing amiss in the spinney. It was dark, though, so he might not have noticed the body. On Sunday he read the church lesson in the morning and played cricket in the afternoon. He doesn't know what made him play the careless stroke that got him out and he was following Zoe across the road because Anne-Marie had told him she was in a mood.

'Then I asked him if he could think of any person who could have any reason to want to kill his father and Mrs Carr answered for him and said they'd discussed it and none of the three of them could understand it. She said that, as with anyone else, there were people who didn't like him but no one who had any reason to wish him dead. Then she "remembered" that her mother needed some medicine. Apparently the hospital discharged her yesterday.'

He stopped walking suddenly and she turned, enquiringly. 'Wouldn't they have supplied her with enough medication for the next few days?' When she nodded, Mitchell looked at his watch. 'We ought to go and report back but I don't feel satisfied with what we've managed this afternoon. Fancy working on our own initiative for an hour?'

She nodded and grinned. 'So long as it's work. I don't want Browne's daughter coming down on me like a ton of bricks.'

'You'd better not let Ginny hear you likening her to a ton of bricks. No, strictly above board.' Their stroll had brought them to the town precinct. 'You pop in there' – he indicated a trendy looking coffee bar – 'and order something long and cold whilst I make a phone call. I assume both kids go to the local comprehensive?'

'Anne-Marie does.'

'Right. Give me five minutes.'

Mr Watmough came to his door, his half glasses in his hand. He escorted the two constables into a small study, put his glasses on a paper-littered desk, offered his visitors chairs, then put his glasses on and peered at them over the semi-circular lenses. Mitchell judged him to be about fifty years old and read in his eyes the opinion that it would be pointless to discuss with someone so near Frank in age the reflections on his pupil of a mature headmaster. Mitchell introduced Jennie, then grinned, disarmingly.

'We grow up fast in this job, sir. At least I was experienced enough to know it would be useful to talk to you. No one sent us.'

Watmough smiled. 'And what has no one sent you to ask me?'

Mitchell supposed this was the sort of question he put to recalcitrant pupils for whom he had a secret soft spot and refused to be mocked. 'Gary Carr has been murdered, sir, as you know. We're not following up any particular lead as yet. It's still very much groundwork. Anything you've heard or observed concerning the matter and in particular concerning the two youngsters might be very useful to us. What are they like from your point of view, especially Frank?'

The glasses were now swinging from Watmough's right hand and he had evidently decided to trust Mitchell with his observations. 'They're both singular children. Frank has caused the more conventional and hidebound of his teachers a certain amount of consternation over the years. His strength and his weakness has been his devastating and unanswerable logic. "Why should I?" was his favourite question, uttered first as an intelligent request for information, and only becoming a defiant protest when it wasn't satisfactorily answered. He didn't find the various paraphrases of "because I say so" very satisfactory and he used to see his teachers as a power-happy band who derived pleasure from making thirty people at once do their pointless bidding. And who's to say he was wrong?

'He's a fine athlete but he used to opt out of organised sport. "What does it matter if I can run faster than Peter," he once asked me, "so long as we can both run fast enough when there's something to run away from?" I'd been taking him to task for laziness after watching him coast along level with the other front runner at a local sports meeting where he was supposedly representing the school. "I don't like burning 'em off, sir," he told me, engagingly. I took his point.'

Mitchell looked puzzled. 'But I thought he was captain of school cricket – and that the county colts were anxious to use him.'

'Yes. His attitude changed as he matured, especially when he entered the sixth form. I know he was rather unhappy and insecure at home. He didn't seem to identify with the family group although he was fond of his mother and sister

77

as individuals. As he made friends at school and was admired for his achievements, academic as well as sporting, he became part of a group and began to appreciate the meaning of group identity.'

Mitchell nodded. 'Thank you, sir. And Anne-Marie?'

The spectacles were reassumed before he spoke. 'Anne-Marie is the sort of child whose conduct is usually described in a school context as exemplary. However, I am glad that her compeers do not follow the example she sets. It worries me when a fifteen-year-old in my school is so biddable, especially when she is so obviously intelligent and imaginative. She's not lacking in initiative either but she always restricts herself to doing, ostentatiously, exactly what she is told.'

'You mean,' Jennie put in, 'that she's been cowed at home and is too timid to take the lead?'

He shook his head vigorously, removing the spectacles for their safety. 'No, not at all. I think she deliberately chooses to behave in that way, though I do think the atmosphere at home has been indirectly responsible. May I ask a question of my own?' They nodded permission. 'They are seventeen and fifteen years old. What would happen to them if either of them were implicated in any way in their father's death?'

Mitchell pondered for a few seconds. 'I don't think any of us could answer that at this stage, sir. It would depend on exactly what they'd done and why. I think I can assure you they'd be dealt with sympathetically, though.'

Watmough sighed. 'Well, whether or not, there are two things I think I ought to tell you. If what I've heard of the matter is true, Carr was killed a week last Tuesday night, and the body was not proven to be his until Tuesday last. There has been something drastically wrong with young Carr since that first Tuesday. He's behaved fairly normally on the surface but for a week and a half now, his concentration and standard of work have fallen off and he hasn't really been himself. I haven't noticed a similar change in his sister. I think either he's done something or he knows something.'

There was a pause of some seconds before Mitchell prompted him. 'Thank you again, sir. And the second thing?'

He answered with obvious reluctance. 'I'm an occasional attender at St Oswald's and several of my pupils were taking part in

78

the pageant last Saturday, so I went along to see it. Very well done indeed. They did Gerald Morgan proud. When I met young Carr in the corridor on Monday morning I wanted to congratulate him on his performance. I said, "I saw you on Saturday night, Carr." I saw the whites of his eyes.'

Chapter 8

The council of war that took place in Browne's office at nine
o'clock that evening was attended with varying degrees of willingness by those he had called. Constable Dean's attitude was
ambivalent. This would be the second time he had broken an
appointment with his new girlfriend but he did have a certain
amount of useful information to offer. Jennie Smith and Mitchell
felt pleased with themselves. They had more to report from the
interview they had initiated than from the one Browne had set
up for them. Bellamy was bored, Hunter excited.

Browne began by ordering coffee for them all and thanking them
for the long stint they were completing and reporting on in person.
Browne's preference for a constable's report of his activities being
made personally was popular rather than otherwise. They realised
that it was partly to get immediate answers to his follow-up
questions, but he was also able to offer immediate commendation
or encouragement. On their part, being asked to detail their own
activities, give their own impression of the people or objects they
had examined, made them feel themselves valued. It did not,
however, let them off any paperwork. Written reports still had
to be made.

Bellamy began with a negative report. No taxi driver or railway
official could give any information on Carr's movements on
Tuesday evening. Dr Christopher Fenwick had confirmed Mrs
Carr's account of her movements from the time of his arrival that
evening at approximately ten o'clock at Mrs Kelly's flat. He had
also interviewed the Ings Lane railway guard who had repeated his
wife's account of the car parked on the track by the spinney on Saturday night but had added no further details. If Bellamy had hoped
to be dismissed once his report was made, he was disappointed.
He subsided on to an upright chair as Dean took his turn.

Mrs Selina James, who lived with her daughter at number sixteen Burnley Brow, had seen Gary Carr leave number nineteen on foot at half-past seven on the night he had supposedly left for Harlow. According to Dean, she was an alert, sharp-eyed eighty-one-year-old who, her daughter assured him, missed very little. Carr had been alone and had gone in the direction of the Rag and Louse. Yes, the Red Lion was nearer but it was in the other direction and Carr didn't drink there. The young lad had come out a few minutes later and gone into the Morgans' house. Mrs James had not seen Carr return but she had seen Mrs Carr go out in her car some time later. She couldn't say what time. And then the young lad had driven Glyn Morgan's car in the same direction. Later still, she'd heard both 'cars' come back. She'd paused to cackle loud and long at the pun. Again, she didn't know the time, but 'a good while after she'd bundled me off to bed', with an indignant nod towards her daughter. She'd heard the Morgans' doorbell ring and the voices of Frank and Anne-Marie, talking quietly as they returned home.

'And she didn't see Carr coming home just after eight?' Browne mused.

Dean shook his head. 'Well, no, sir. But after a few minutes I asked her what she'd been watching on television that night and she described the programmes in such detail with such scathing comments that she must have been looking at the screen most of the time. On the other hand she didn't miss much whilst she was talking to me. She paid attention to my questions and answered promptly, but every time there was the slightest noise from outside, her eyes slid to the window till she knew what caused it. She said Mr Priestley's van had been parked outside number nineteen a lot recently whilst Carr was out but she assured me that the children were in and everything very proper. Mr Priestley visits Mrs James often and is "a nice gentleman and can't be blamed for Mr Carr spending so much time at the pub".'

Browne nodded. 'Did you try the Rag and Louse?'

'Yes, sir, but I didn't learn much that we didn't know or suspect already. The landlord played in the church cricket match and we went through it almost ball by ball before I could get him on to anything else. He doesn't think much of Carr and he thinks even less of Gerald Morgan. Said he batted number three because his expertise would be demonstrated to

81

better effect if it had been preceded by some ham-fisted slog-ging.'

'You're not giving me a verbatim report?'

Dean smiled at this tribute to his neat phraseology. 'No, sir.'

'Try to give me more of a flavour of the landlord.'

Dean bridled. 'Sir. Carr would go in and order a half and make it last. I said if he was out of work he wouldn't be able to afford to get involved in rounds. Poskitt, that's the landlord, said, "Aye, but 'e wouldn't if 'e could if yer see what I mean. Yer can pick out an open-'anded chap even when 'e's nowt ter give." '

Browne realised that he was being mocked and was lenient with Dean because he disliked him. 'Would you summarise, briefly, the rest of the interview?'

Glad to have been let off, Dean complied. 'Carr used to sit in a corner by himself mostly. At least he didn't hang on to a group and drink at their expense. Poskitt said he'd only ever seen him drunk once and that was quite recently. He was with that young chap, Atkinson, who's moved in with the religious nut, Priestley. When Glyn Morgan persuaded him to go home, Poskitt was disapproving. He was talking nonsense but not causing any trouble and he might have spent more than when he was sober.'

'This incident wasn't the same evening that Carr disappeared?'

'No. To get back to that, Carr came in at about seven forty-five and a phone call came for him at five past eight or thereabouts. After the grandfather clock that's the pride of Poskitt's life had struck anyway. It was a woman's voice and Poskitt handed over the receiver and asked Carr to make it quick because he was busy. Carr spoke to his caller briefly, then drained his glass and said he had to go. Poskitt wasn't desolated. He'd already served Carr as much as he usually ordered and his company was depressing. He can't say which direction Carr took, but one of the bar staff did notice, through the window, that he stopped and spoke to someone. She wasn't sure who it was, one of several people who were just arriving and who came in a crowd. She can only remember one of them, Walter Crossley. That was because he was playing in Saturday's cricket match and she knew he and Poskitt would stand either side of the bar for an hour or more having yet another boring discussion of their chances against the under-twenty-fives whilst she ran her legs into the ground serving.

'The next bit was interesting. Just seconds before the bell rang

82

for last orders, Theresa Carr came in. Frank was with her but he remained in the doorway. She came up to the bar and asked Poskitt if he'd seen a silver ball-point pen that Carr had misplaced. She said it had been a birthday present from her mother to him and, as there wasn't much love lost between them, he'd better not make things worse by losing her gift. He could remember fiddling with it whilst drinking his half and wondered if he'd left it on the table. It wasn't there. She chatted for a few minutes, telling Poskitt about the job in Harlow, then apologised for repeating it when he'd probably heard it all from her husband. Poskitt said no, Carr had gone straight out after receiving the call without speaking to anyone. Then both Carrs left. He thought it must be a valuable pen for two of them to be seeking it at eleven o'clock at night.'

Browne nodded. 'Good work, Dean. That's interesting. So Mr Priestley's boyfriend was with Carr on the only occasion anyone ever saw him the worse for drink. I wonder what they talked about. Right, you two, you can spill your beans now before the bag bursts.'

Mitchell briefly summarised their interviews with the young Carrs, stressing the mother's determination to protect Frank. Then, with increased enthusiasm, they described their session with Mr Watmough. Indignation fought with astonishment when Browne administered a sharp rebuke.

'When I want you to organise my investigation, Mitchell, I'll ask. Until then, just do as you are told.'

'You did say you trusted their discretion, sir, and they have come up with something useful.' To his astonishment, Browne realised the remark had come from Hunter.

Pushing his advantage, Mitchell added, 'Sergeant Hunter looks as though he's on to something, too.'

Browne capitulated and nodded to Hunter to continue.

'Well, sir, Frank Carr has worked Saturdays at the garage in Archer Road since Christmas. The manager says if he wanted a permanent job he'd give him one tomorrow. He's punctual, reliable, polite and learns fast. His boss often leaves him now to diagnose a problem and deal with it on his own initiative so long as there's someone around to ask when he gets stuck. Carr senior has worked there on odd occasions, usually with dire results. On the last occasion he was given a service to do, including an oil change. He remembered to drain the sump but not to fill it up again. Later that day, the customer's engine seized up. Cost the firm an arm and a leg. He wouldn't have worked there again.'

Browne looked puzzled. 'Is that all? You had your broody look. I thought you were on to something.'

'I am. You remember that scrap of heavy-duty polythene we found in the spinney? This same firm has a contract to service NHS wheelchairs and vehicles specially adapted for the disabled in this area. When a chair is ready for delivery back to its owner it's protected in transit in a huge yellow polythene bag with "Cloughton Health Authority" printed in black letters.'

Browne rewarded all this industry by making his own contribution. 'Want to hear the path lab report? It would have been fascinating if we were still trying to make an identification. As it is, the only interesting fact is that Carr was poisoned with nicotine.'

His listeners digested this information in a silence which Browne allowed to continue for a minute or two whilst he usurped Hunter's place at the window. The landscape to the north of the town lay before him in the fading light, ill-used but unashamed in all its scruffy splendour. The ancient parish church stood submerged in the valley, showing only its clock and the pinnacles on the base of its spire above huge blocks of old mill buildings which had been converted into the new industrial estate. At first, Browne had hated its rows of symmetrical flat windows in walls of shiny-clean millstone grit from which had been sandblasted away the smoke deposits that had once belched from the redundant chimneys. Now he was becoming fond of it again. In spite of clean air regulations, the activities of the town's new industries were laying a further patina of grime and making the area look well used and grubby again. Tower blocks of flats rose from the lower slopes of the far valley side, 'eyesores' according to Hunter, but Browne accepted them. They were functional; people had to live somewhere. They contributed to the friendly huddle that was Cloughton.

In the immediate foreground were two horse boxes waiting to return the animals used to control the crowd at that afternoon's demonstration against the poll tax. Halters hung on the lower inside doors. From where Browne stood, it seemed that, if the driver inched forward, his vehicle would plunge down the steep grassy slope on which the station was built. Cloughton's demonstration had been orderly. The town had nothing to offer to the troublesome gangs from the big cities only a few miles away and they mostly left it alone. Cars on the main road below the roughly cut grass bank beneath Browne's window roared to and from Leeds, Bradford and the M62, unheeding.

Presently, he turned back into the room. 'Where does all that get us? Bellamy?'

Bellamy shook himself awake and scowled ferociously. 'The barmaid at the Rag and Louse had the last sighting of Carr that we can rely on,' he began. 'Someone needs to see her again to press her about who Carr spoke to as he left the pub.' The scowl continued but not his list of suggestions.

'Dean?'

'It sounded to me, sir, as though Mrs Carr made up the pen story so that she could go back to the pub and check up on what her husband had said before he left.'

Mitchell cut in. 'Do we accept that the phone call at the pub came from her? Poskitt told Richard that it was a woman's voice.' Dean nodded. 'And Poskitt played in the church cricket match,' Mitchell continued, 'so that presumably means he attended St O's and was at least acquainted with Theresa Carr?' He glanced at Hunter for confirmation. 'So, if she'd rung, wouldn't she have identified herself to him and wouldn't he have recognised her voice?'

Browne scribbled. Hunter suspected he was making notes on each of his team's contribution to the discussion, rather than on the progress of the case. After a minute he looked up. 'Good thinking. Anything to add, Jerry?'

'We've some more interviewing to do. Theresa Carr's connections with Priestley and Morgan had better be looked into. And the other Morgans live in the best position to have seen anything there was to see, although they won't want to tell any tales, especially Christine. And I'm beginning to think you're right about Priestley's – er – friend. Someone should have a word with him about his connection with Carr.'

With a few words of thanks and appreciation of both their industry and their ideas, Browne dismissed them to the rest they all felt they deserved. His satisfaction to be going home had no reservations. Since their agreement that Virginia should have twelve months to work out what she really wanted to do with her life, peace and goodwill had reigned. He was enjoying the case, too, more than any since he had been promoted to inspector. His sergeant's involvement, socially, with the protagonists gave him a good excuse to be out on the job with them more than was approved of by his superiors. Jerry could interview Fenwick and probably Monica Kelly but there were cogent arguments for keeping him, in his official capacity, away from both Morgans, Priestley and the vicar and for Browne talking to them himself. He was slightly niggled by the amount of time that was passing since the last day in July when, very likely, Carr had been poisoned, but they'd had to identify the body before any search for his killer could begin. Tomorrow he would have a long session with the Morgans, who had been dealt with only cursorily. Bellamy could see Priestley's partner, Charles Atkinson, and, if she were well enough, Jerry could have a talk with Monica Kelly.

The fresh sparkle of the next morning's sun had relieved Browne's journey through the estate of little boxes which clung grimly to the slope below him. Each dwelling was tiny yet ostentatious. Browne imagined that the vocabulary of the vending agents would have included 'compact' and 'bijou'. Tiny lawns alternated with tarmacked drives just the width of a small car. The slope of the land made steps from the gardens up to the front doors necessary on this side of the road but, edged with white painted railings which continued along the tiny platforms in front of the doors, the flights seemed ridiculously pretentious. The lawns seemed even smaller than they were because in the centre of most was a pathetic sapling, dwarfed by its stake. This was probably just as well, since any self-respecting tree in that position would soon heave up the house's foundations. Browne willed just one of the trees to make it to maturity, though doubtless, if this happened, the undiscriminating owner would have the tree rather than the house demolished.

Round the Carrs' house, a combination of drainpipes and tubes to carry away central heating fumes made it look like a post-operative patient. In front of number twenty-one, the Morgans', the ground fell away still more sharply, so that the steps up to it turned and continued in the opposite direction, giving scope for a much greater expanse of white railing. Not so many pipes coiled around this house but a collection of thin metal chimneys sticking out of the roof looked like candles on a birthday cake. Browne shook his head impatiently at these fancies but wondered why people couldn't build houses that looked like houses. Dwarf conifers round the Morgans' lawn added to the toytown effect. He thought his prejudice against arborial Alpine refugees was justified. They looked healthy enough at the moment but, before September was out, the wind would whistle down the valley and burn off all the needles.

On the opposite side of the road the gardens dropped down from the pavement and a man who was locking the boot of his car before going into his house would have to peer over his low hedge of berberis to find it. The cars of the other houses on the man's side showed him their rumps and coyly hid their faces under the carports and garages that received them from the precipitous drives. Browne did not envy their owners who would have to reverse them out on icy mornings.

Towering scornfully on the rising hillside beyond was a row of 'proper' houses, a Victorian terrace of red brick, two up and two down, but with dignity, roomy attics, substantial chimney pots and roofs of slate, not corrugated pottery in Noddy colours. Half a dozen plots further down, the builders seemed to have run out of either materials or energy. The road petered out into a stony wasteland upon which grass was once more encroaching and, beyond, a magnificent bank of rocky ground rose, heather-covered, towards which the railway viaduct hurdled its way across the intervening valley.

Browne lowered his eyes again to the estate of houses. The multitude of small differences introduced by the builder combined to emphasise their sameness. He climbed the steps to the Morgans' front door. The platform in front of it was too small for two and Mitchell had to remain behind him on the steps. As Browne waited for his ring to be answered, he remembered Philip Garside's assurance of this family's integrity and had a feeling he could rely on this judgement.

Zoe was as eager as Browne for the police to interview her family, and since the phone call last night that fixed this morning's appointment, she had awaited it with good humour sufficient to help her mother by removing her possessions from the otherwise spotless and orderly living room. She paused in her progress upstairs, shifted the weight of a pile of pop magazines to her other hip and leaned over the banister. 'You have to laugh at the idea of Jerry Hunter being the fuzz. Can you just see him, sorting out drunks on a Saturday night or frogmarching football hooligans?' A burst of laughter carried her to her room, where she tossed the magazines on to her bed.

Christine Morgan had equal difficulty imagining this. 'I don't think the CID do things like that. I agree he does look more like a lawyer,' she allowed. She carried a tray with the breakfast dishes through to the kitchen.

Zoe, who had come downstairs again, followed her. 'Not the sort that makes speeches in court, though. More like the stuffy ones who pore over documents in gloomy offices. Or a poet, maybe.' She obviously considered the latter to be sinking even lower.

Her mother stacked pots on the draining board. 'He certainly reads poetry.'

Zoe, feeling magnanimous, grabbed a tea cloth. 'He would. He's pretty snobby, like his wife.'

'You shouldn't use that word as a general term for people you don't like,' her mother admonished mildly. 'He isn't a social snob though he may be an intellectual one. He's certainly a little old-fashioned. I don't know how he'll cope if Felicity turns into a teenager like you.'

Zoe was scornful. 'She hasn't a hope!'

Christine thought Zoe was very probably right. 'Anyway, it wasn't Sergeant Hunter who rang. It was Chief Inspector Browne.'

'The little dark one with the snapping eyes? I've talked to him already. You can't mess him about but he looks as though he could take a joke. One of the young ones is really dishy. He's called Nigel. I'm not interested though. I don't want to muck Frank about just now. Where's he gone anyway? I thought he was going to change our tyres this morning. He buzzed off as soon as he heard the rozzers were on their way. Oh well, he's had his grilling already. I don't suppose he wants another one. And it's not much fun having your father murdered I suppose, even if you did hate him.'

'Zoe!'

Unabashed, Zoe wandered to the window. 'They're here now.'

'Zoe, come away from the window.'

She remained. 'I don't see why I should. They're having a good gawp at our place, their eyes are all over the shop. He hasn't brought the dishy one. It's the other fattish one who's almost as small as he is.'

Christine sighed. 'If you must feast your eyes on them, go and let them in, and for goodness' sake be polite.'

Zoe escorted the two officers through a small hall that led, by two steps and an archway, straight into the living room. The steps were probably in the original plan of the house, made necessary by the steepness of the ground, but Browne suspected that Christine Morgan had suggested the removal of the door and frame and the building of the wide arch through which a comfortably furnished sitting area could be seen. He had an impression of creams, browns and apricots, merging subtly, and registered sharply a set of bookshelves which were suspended from the ceiling. He was prevented from his usual ploy of forming an opinion of the members of a household by the titles of the books it displayed. Trailing ivies on the top shelf gracefully obliterated the titles and suggested that the books were chosen for their attractive bindings and were not often removed.

Christine Morgan took charge of the interview and at this point it suited Browne to let her. She despatched her daughter to her own quarters upstairs and saw that Browne and Mitchell were made equally comfortable in cream leather chairs. Then she seated herself ready for their questions. Browne studied her. She was extremely well groomed but her careful make-up emphasised her chief characteristic which was ordinariness. And yet she had the same – Browne sought the word – not serenity, more of an inner confidence, as her daughter. Her clothes were casual and expensive looking but the button-through summer dress, white necklace and stud earrings were too conventional to be elegant and the cap sleeves were wrong, not only for her plump arms but for the 'attractive mature woman' image that she had otherwise achieved. Browne refused her offer of coffee and asked for an account of her movements and observations on the night of Gary Carr's disappearance.

She confirmed Frank's visit and the wildlife video he had watched with Zoe. Yes, Zoe was genuinely interested in it and so was Frank. Theresa had rung towards the end of it and asked to speak to Frank about the car. She couldn't have said what time that was if she'd been asked the same day and she certainly couldn't remember it now. They'd lent Frank their own car in case he couldn't put his mother's right and he'd departed in it. Around ten, Anne-Marie had arrived at the door and had been collected at about eleven. She was sorry to be vague but she hadn't known the times would be important.

Mitchell scribbled. Browne thanked her and leaned back in his chair. 'Could I possibly change my mind and accept that offer of coffee?'

Mitchell, who had got up too late for any breakfast, was considerably cheered. The coffee had obviously been made in advance and the filter machine left on. In a couple of minutes it was being dispensed from a tray together with chocolate biscuits. Whilst his hostess's hands were still busy, Browne asked, casually, 'Could you take us through the festival weekend from your point of view, with all your impressions, however little they seem to have to do with the case? Begin with the choir practice on Friday evening.' He helped himself to sugar, then leaned back in his chair, stirring carefully.

She cast her mind back to the rather fraught rehearsal and described her husband's tetchy manner during this last run-through of his composition. Zoe had been nervous too and had gone back to making the mistakes her father had patiently coached her out of during earlier sessions. The parents of the younger choristers, anxious to get them home and to bed, had become impatient, and Zoe, aware of this, had begun to sing sharp. Her father had realised that things were not going to improve and called a halt to the proceedings. Christine had come forward, flapping her arms against her sides, and congratulated Annette on the striking flower arrangements. 'I think they're even better than last year and you did us proud then.' She had blown on her fingers. 'It's freezing in here, however hot it is outside but at least it will keep the flowers fresh till the festivities are over. It's worth coming to the services just to see them.'

Feeling that something was due from her, Annette had done her duty. 'Zoe sang beautifully tonight. You must be really proud of her.' Then, worried that Fliss, who was too young to know better, might repeat some of the strictures on Zoe's appearance, manners and morals that she had overheard at home, Annette beamed, said good night and hustled her children outside. Well aware of

90

Annette's true feelings about her daughter, Christine had smiled and she smiled again as she remembered.

On Saturday morning she had been busy with household matters and had seen nothing of the Carrs or the church. In the afternoon, she had attended the Sunday School concert and had noticed nothing more amiss than that the singing was flat. Anne-Marie had helped with the little ones but both Zoe and Frank had refused to attend. They had, however, gone to the last briefing for the pageant which had followed, leaving her in peace to prepare tea. The pageant had been a huge success. She had had nothing to do with the organisation of it but had helped with refreshments in the kitchen. The women had been too busy to talk, except about whether the buns would go round and the milk last out. Then they'd all gone back to Theresa's house as previously arranged. Christine's brow wrinkled. 'I had half an impression that she didn't want us. We were all shot at. We didn't stay long.'

'Had Mrs Carr managed to sort out her smelly drain?' Browne turned in astonishment at Mitchell's question.

'Oh, did she tell you about that?' Christine remembered sniffing as she entered Theresa's hall that night and asking a similar question as she noticed the absence of the peculiar sweetish smell that had been worrying Theresa the previous day.

'We found a dead rat in the cellar.' Frank had spoken abruptly and loudly, startling the two women who had been unaware of his quiet presence.

His mother had been faintly embarrassed. 'Don't let the whole neighbourhood know, Frank. It's not exactly something to be proud of. It shows we don't clear out the cellar often enough.' She had turned back to Christine. 'I think it's that young Jack Russell they've acquired next door. It probably had a go at the poor thing before it escaped to die in our cellar. We've buried it now.'

Christine had been looking through the window as she listened. 'The dog's there in your drive. It's having a good sniff round the boot of your car. It hasn't chased one in there too, has it?' Theresa had come to see for herself.

Frank had contributed another loud statement. 'We gave my friend a lift to the vet with his dog – or bitch rather. She's on heat. That isn't the first dog to show an interest in the car since. It's getting dark now but I'll give it a good clean-out tomorrow first thing.'

His mother, who had looked rather disconcerted at his intervention, had pulled out a chair. 'Come and sit where we can see you, then we won't jump out of our skins every time you say something. How are you getting on with the team?'

'I'm still a man short.' He had declined the seat but offered the list he had made for his mother's inspection, then hovered in the doorway, one foot hooked round the other, trying to find an excuse to depart without seeming rude. His mother had taken pity on him. 'Would you and Zoe mind making the coffee for us before you disappear?'

'Surely.'

They had departed, promptly and thankfully, and Theresa had smiled at Christine. 'Poor Frank. He isn't out of his chrysalis yet. Everything he says is either too loud or too crudely phrased and his own embarrassment makes everyone else feel awkward. Girls slip into the social graces much more easily.'

Christine had grimaced. 'Like Zoe, you mean?'

She finished her story and looked up at Browne. 'Things like drains always go wrong when there's no man around to cope. But Theresa and Frank are independent. They didn't want any help.'

Mitchell looked up from his scribbling to shoot a triumphant glance at Browne. Browne ignored it and renewed his questioning. 'Tell me about Mrs Carr's relationship with her mother.'

Christine looked relieved. This was safe ground, though not easy to explain. 'It's complicated. Mrs Kelly's an obnoxious woman. Theresa's her only child and she looks on her life and Anne-Marie's too as second and third chances for herself. She thinks she should make all their decisions for them and she doesn't think Theresa has a right to any privacy. If she's alone in their house, she reads their letters and private things. They know because when she's off guard she lets fall bits of information that she shouldn't know and then insists that one of them told her. Only a couple of weeks ago, Anne-Marie lost her diary and it turned up in Mrs Kelly's handbag. She must have been disturbed when she was reading it and put it in there. Then she forgot to put it back where she'd found it before she went home. Theresa found out because her mother asked for her reading glasses to be brought to the hospital and the handbag was where she said they would be. She doesn't even keep what she's found out to herself. She broadcasts their business around just as it suits her. Fortunately, what she's chiefly interested in is how much they paid for everything and, although it's annoying not to have the choice, Theresa doesn't mind people knowing that sort of thing. She's a dreadful snob. Mrs Kelly, I mean.'

Christine began to gather cups on to a tray and her thoughts together again. When both were neatly arranged, she turned back to Browne. 'People who only meet Theresa at work would never believe the hold Mrs Kelly has over her. She's so efficient and handles the patients so deftly it's hard to understand why she can't use the same methods with her mother. The Catholics know, though. Don't they say if you can have a child and teach it for the first seven years, they'll give it up and know it will always hold to what they've taught it? Mrs Kelly never encouraged Theresa to express or assert herself. The sort of paralysis she felt when she was scorned or criticised or ordered around was her instinctive reaction that she couldn't fight against or control. She has plenty of spirit in the areas of her life that her mother has never entered, but in the relationship between the two of them Theresa seems to have been permanently warped.'

Browne was having difficulty reconciling these penetrating observations with the conventionally respectable looking woman in front of him. Then he remembered that she had brought up Zoe. 'Are these your own thoughts or has Mrs Carr talked to you about her feelings?'

Christine considered. 'A bit of both really. We've had many a heart-to-heart in front of her fire or mine since we became neighbours, but I've watched the old woman manipulating her too.' Suddenly she chuckled. 'She resents me – Mrs Kelly, I mean – because Theresa values my opinion. And she heartily disapproves of her grandson's liaison with Zoe.' A sudden surge of pop music from upstairs had obviously brought her daughter to mind. 'Theresa was always stifled by the rigid, timid, smug respectability she was raised into. When she met Gary I think she found his devil-may-care enjoyment of life quite irresistible, but then somehow it all went sour. I'm sure Mrs Kelly was responsible for it. Gary felt he didn't have Theresa's first loyalty and Mrs

Kelly's constant, carping criticism seemed to wither him because he felt Theresa was on her mother's side. In the end, Theresa seemed to gain a fair capacity to enjoy life, at least when her mother wasn't around, and Gary lost it. He was always a bit weak and irresponsible.' She paused.

'Tell me more about Gary,' Browne encouraged her.

There was a long pause, during which she looked down at her hands. 'I could never quite make up my mind about him. He wasn't generally liked because he was moody. Theresa was' – she paused again as she sought the word she wanted and brought it out triumphantly – 'ensnared by him. She believed at first that a set of circumstances would turn up one day that would allow the best side of him to show and develop. He wasn't a very good father. Inconsistent people aren't are they? He enjoyed indulging his children until they irritated him and then he'd let fly at them. Frank got resentful and very protective of Theresa and his sister. Anne-Marie remained vulnerable. She enjoyed the petting and then got hysterically upset when her father lost his temper with her. She usually flew off to be comforted by Mrs Kelly and God knows what harm *she* did to the situation. Most people think Theresa is well rid of Gary but she's really grieving for him. She feels she was just beginning to resist her mother and to see that Gary has been a victim of her alternately spoiling him and then putting him second in her life. She had great plans for getting herself together and trying to normalise their relationship.'

Wondering how Mitchell might have recorded this insight into Theresa Carr's affairs, Browne gave him an easier task by recalling his witness to the night Carr had disappeared and asking her which of her neighbours' movements she had observed through the window. Her answers were disappointing. She had watched the wildlife film with the young folk and then cooked the supper in the kitchen at the back of the house.

When Browne asked to see Zoe, Christine surprised him again. 'Never mind what my rights are. She'll tell you more if I'm not there. I'm certain neither Theresa nor Zoe has done anything to be worried about or ashamed of and I'm anxious for you to find out as much as possible. Theresa hasn't a hope of putting her life back together until your job's finished.' She directed him to Zoe's room. 'Follow the noise.'

Browne began to explain that even with her explicit permission, he was not allowed to accept this offer. He agreed, though, to talk to Zoe in her own room, where she would feel more relaxed. The doorbell rang to announce the welcome arrival of Jennie Smith before Mrs Morgan led the way upstairs.

Chapter 9

The noise of four pairs of feet carrying, in Mitchell's case at least, a not inconsiderable weight up the stairs was blotted out by the clamour that issued from a room on the landing with the door ajar. Browne could see Zoe sitting on the bed, wielding a hairbrush that rendered her more dishevelled with every stroke. Only when, out of the corner of her eye, she noticed their movements in the doorway did she become aware of them. She laid the brush on the bed but continued to sit for a few seconds, making no physical response to the music, as though, somewhere in the middle of the din, she had found a centre of stillness.

Suddenly she grinned at them, signalled an invitation to enter and reached out an arm to switch off the tape recorder on the bedside table. Browne noted with satisfaction that she had pressed the Stop button rather than the one marked Pause. Evidently she was going to take her questioning seriously. With aplomb she offered him the only armchair and moved to the end of the bed to make room for his underlings. Her mother unobtrusively occupied herself tidying the bookshelves.

Browne had expected to find Zoe in jeans and a tee-shirt but she was wearing a well-cut dress in a wrapover style, belted tightly to emphasise her full bust and tiny waistline. It was in a bright kingfisher blue which a deep tan helped her to carry off. This girl's attire would always make a statement. As she grew older it would become more subtle and she would make an even greater impression. Huge earrings adorned neat ears, white enamelled hoops which must have seriously inconvenienced if not actually pained her. The rough cap of sun-bleached hair contrasted with a peach bloom skin and the full lips did not exactly pout but they could have done if her mood had required it. She had a snub nose and nicely arched brows over eyes that were sometimes challenging but at the moment just interested. Browne couldn't decide whether she was pretty or whether her self-confidence projected an image of prettiness through the features she happened to have.

Jennie Smith, having settled herself on the pillow side of Zoe, leaned against them, kicking off her shoes and tucking her feet beneath her. She glanced at Browne for permission to open the proceedings and received an affirming nod. 'Is this Shaun Shannon's latest?' she asked, picking up the empty cassette case from the bedside table.

Zoe grinned amiably at her. 'You don't have to chat me up, you know, or pretend to be interested. That's from his first album and it's been out of the charts for more than a year but it's still my favourite. Let's get the questions over and I'll lend it to you when you go.'

Mitchell enjoyed Jennie's discomfiture until Browne caught his eye and invited him to continue. Zoe intercepted the glances they exchanged and her own challenged Mitchell boldly.

Unabashed he decided on the direct approach. 'Do you know anything about all this, Zoe? You're observant. Did you see or hear anything that would help us to prove people's innocence as well as guilt? Tell us everything you can think of and then no one will have any reason to try to stop you talking.'

She saw at once what he meant and addressed him solemnly. 'I honestly can't tell you anything that seems to me to be of any use, but I'll tell you as much as I can about whatever you ask.'

'Fair enough.' Browne took his turn and by tacit agreement the interview took the form of an adolescent pow-wow with all three officers chipping in informally. 'Take us through last weekend then please, beginning with the choir practice and ending with the first part of the cricket match. Don't just give us the bare facts. Tell us what you noticed and what you thought about.'

She nodded. 'Well, the practice went quite well at first. We had a quick run through the psalms and the sung parts of the service. Then we started on the anthem and Dad got in a foul mood. We hadn't really practised it enough. I think it was because he'd written it and if we worked at it too often or he was too fussy about it everybody would think he was showing off. Anyway, I kept getting my solo wrong. Dad kept saying, "Just a minute, Zoe, it's a minor not a major third as you come down the arpeggio in bar twenty." He said it so often that the choirboys were chanting it with him and I could feel everybody in the row behind glaring at my back because they wanted to go home. Why are descending scales so much harder to sing than going up?'

Browne shook his head. 'I wouldn't know. I can't sing scales of any description.'

'Lucky you!' she told him with feeling. 'I was supposed to kneel down for the first part – you know, "that we may bear reproach and persecution" – but I wouldn't.' Browne raised an enquiring eyebrow, not suspecting religious scruples. Zoe explained. 'Alan Priestley once told us in Sunday School years ago that if we cared a little about something, God cared about it a hundred times more. By that reckoning, I thought He must be pretty worried about me scraping the toes of my new shoes.'

Browne was amused. 'What was more to the point, did your father care?'

She tossed her head. 'I told him I couldn't get enough breath to sing a top A in that position. In the end, Dad gave up trying to get it right and told us to pack up. Then, Annette Hunter, silly cow, started sniffing because I wasn't wearing a bra and she could see my nipples through my tee-shirt. What's wrong with nipples, for goodness' sake. Hasn't she got any?' Browne knew if he stemmed the flow of Zoe's vigorous opinions he would dry up the vital drops of information that someone more circumspect mightn't give him. He sat back to continue listening but Zoe was casting sly glances at Mitchell, hoping she'd embarrassed him.

Poker-faced, he was dutifully writing in his notebook. Jennie grinned at Zoe in sympathy. She had suffered similar strictures in her own not-distant adolescence, usually from narrow-minded, broad-hipped ladies, whose bodies swelled below the waist rather than above, half restrained by unflatteringly stretched crimplene. 'What happened when the practice was over? Did you go straight home?'

Zoe turned to her and nodded. 'No, I went to the pub with Frank but we came back early. On Saturday morning I helped at home, making scones for the cricket match tea because Frank was working. He's a brill mechanic. Not like his dad. He worked at the same place once. He made a right balls-up that cost the firm a new engine in somebody's car. That man in Harlow who sent for him must have been pretty desperate, or else Mr Carr's gone downhill a lot since he used to work with his friend. That's if he was really going to a job in Harlow and it wasn't all a story.' The three officers pricked up their ears. 'Anne-Marie says he went away once before and was supposed to be working but he was really living with another woman. I didn't believe her. She's always making up stories and she gets so involved with them, she ends up believing them herself. She said if her father was with another woman he might get AIDS and if he gave that to her mother she'd kill him.' As she realised what she'd said, Zoe's eyes widened and she fell silent.

Jennie asked, 'Are you friendly with Anne-Marie?'

'I suppose so.'

'Well, are you or not?'

She considered. 'I never really think about her like that. She's just somebody who needs to be looked after. She's too odd for you to ask yourself normal questions like whether you like her or not.' She gave a rueful grin. 'She'd say I was her friend but I'm not always very nice to her.'

Mitchell raised his eyes from his notebook. 'What about Saturday afternoon?'

'Well, that's a good example. She wanted Frank and me to watch the Sunday School concert because she was helping but we made an excuse. Frank mucked about with their car and I made coffee – and things.' They spared her blushes.

'But you went to the pageant rehearsal?'

'Yes. Frank was St Aidan and I was helping with the props. We both went home for tea afterwards and Anne-Marie was sulking so I had mine here. We had to be back for half-past six and we were all in the church hall getting ready. Annie had stopped sulking by then so I did her make-up for her. She wouldn't look half bad if she used it properly. The pageant was really good, especially Annie's part. She's a quiet little mouse most of the time but she's good at acting. She speaks and moves differently and she even looks decent. Everybody clapped for ages. Frank and I went for a walk in the spinney afterwards.' She bit her lip. 'You don't want to know about that do you?'

Browne shook his head. 'Only to ask if you're certain Mr Carr's body wasn't then where you saw it later.'

'I'm certain.'

'You went to the Carrs' house for supper?'

'For coffee. Mum thought they wanted rid of us so we only stayed a short while.'

Mitchell asked, 'What did you do then?'

'At home? Went to bed. It was quite late, about midnight.'

Jennie unfolded her cramped legs. 'Did you fall asleep straight away?'

'I did when everybody had finished slamming car doors and driving about. Whoever it was was trying to be quiet, but you lie awake longer, being nosy and wondering who it is, than if they shout and you know you're not missing anything important. It sounded quite close. I'd have thought it was the Carrs if I hadn't known they'd just gone to bed.'

Zoe had fallen asleep without listening for the car to return. Sunday morning had been as usual, all the high jinks being reserved for the Festal Evensong. Frank had read the lesson and Anne-Marie had sung 'Jesus wants me for a sunbeam' whilst Zoe had blushed for her. Sunday afternoon had been a total disaster. She had dropped her Walkman as they set out for the cricket match so it wouldn't work and Frank had been so absorbed in his silly match he'd ignored her even in the interval. Asked about July 31st she declared that all she could remember was how annoyed she'd been when the video had been interrupted by Theresa's phone call to Frank. Her father had answered it to begin with and Frank had rushed off in his car.

'Your turn to sulk?' Mitchell asked.

Zoe bridled. 'I'd specially recorded that programme for Frank to watch. He's doing A level zoology. I thought Mrs Kelly had probably made Theresa ring just because she'd found out that Frank was with me. She thinks Theresa and Frank and Anne-Marie are three servants for her. If she had her way, she'd move in with them and they could wait on her all the time. She might just do that now that Mr Carr isn't there to stop her.'

'Had there been arguments about it?'

Zoe shrugged. 'Not exactly. Mrs Kelly never says anything straight out so you can't argue with her. When she wants any of them to do something she says it's for their own good or they owe it to her or it's what anyone would expect. And if they do what she wants she isn't satisfied. When she moved into her flat she grumbled about having to get rid of some of her furniture. She didn't want it to go out of the family, so Theresa took it for

100

her even though it didn't fit in at all with her own stuff. Frank got lumbered with a great, old-fashioned wardrobe that spoils his room.'

She looked with satisfaction round her own. She had obviously been given her head when it was furnished. There was no sign of the soft textures and pastel colours prevalent throughout the rest of the house. One wall was plastered with posters, wild animal photographs vying for pride of place with gyrating pop stars. The other three were stark white, the one opposite the window adorned with red plastic inflated cushions in the shape of lips. The chair and bookshelves had frames of red tubular steel and the duvet cover on which three of them were sitting had black and red stripes. The carpet was plain black. If he had seen the room empty, Browne would have presumed its occupant to be a boy rather than a girl.

Zoe was chattering on. 'That didn't satisfy her. She said it was funny they could find room for her valuable furniture but not for her. She just loves to have something to grumble about. Frank and Annie took me round to see her flat when she first moved in and she made us some tea. Frank offered to wash up but she said no, she'd rather he chatted to her. Then, when he'd gone out to fetch our coats, she said to me, "He didn't want twice telling to leave those dishes, did he?" You're supposed to insist on helping till it looks mean of her to refuse – as though she's doing you a favour, letting you do it.'

Browne recognised the code of conduct of another generation but he didn't think he could get Zoe to understand. He had been hoping she would chatter more freely about Frank Carr but thought it wiser at this stage not to question her directly about him. He thanked her for being so helpful and the three officers descended the stairs. Glyn Morgan, his wife informed them, was to be found in church making some adjustments to the organ which would take at least the rest of the morning. Browne decided to talk to him there and possibly to have another word with the vicar.

He paused at the gate to reassemble his forces.

'The girl's a hard little nut,' Jennie observed. 'You'd think finding a charred and rotting corpse would upset a sixteen-year-old for quite some time, especially when it turns out to be her boyfriend's father. She wasn't just calm and collected, she was in the best of spirits.'

Browne smiled. 'Most youngsters are equally resilient. She was pretty shaken when it first happened. She almost joked about it when she reported it to Sergeant Hunter because that was a way of avoiding the reality of it. And from her point of view it's no great tragedy. She isn't mature enough to see below the surface of Frank's criticism of his father to the almost reluctant affection he felt for him. Few of us feel deeply for long about things that don't concern us directly and this girl is honest enough not to pretend to.'

As they left, he noticed Theresa Carr hovering at the top of her drive. Before the car had turned the corner she had disappeared into the Morgans' house.

Chapter 10

As he entered the church Browne speculated about the small white discs with numbers on them, screwed to the ends of the pews. The building had been well filled for the Evensong he had attended but the days were gone when reservations had to be made and seats allocated to the congregation's different families.

He felt alien in this weekday church. His footsteps made no sound on the thick carpet in the aisle. They would have been drowned in any case by the disembodied music that reverberated in the black and white rafters and between the stone pillars of the nave. The stained glass window over the Communion Table turned the ordinary sunlight into a Victorian illumination. It was a scene prepared (as the setting) for communication between God and His people, not an acting chief detective inspector and a less than accomplished organist.

He moved forward to the chancel steps from where the organist could be seen, silhouetted against the floodlit music stand. He had become visible himself in the organ mirror, causing Morgan to stop playing and switch off the light. A slim pair of legs in grey canvas jeans and trainers appeared, then the rest of him as he swung himself easily over the back choir pew from the organ loft. 'I'm sorry,' he began. 'I didn't know whether you'd want to see me. I was out on the Tuesday evening that Gary went missing and the Carrs are more Christine's and Zoe's friends than mine.'

Browne ignored this odd reasoning and, after shaking hands, the two men settled into the front pew with Mitchell perched on the one behind. He sat fidgeting whilst Browne went through some initial pleasantries with his witness. Churches were foreign territory to Mitchell and he soon resolved to let them remain so. The hollow acoustics, which seemed to echo even the sound of his breathing, made him uneasy. The thin strip of carpet on the

103

oak beneath him failed to protect him even marginally from its hardness and it let through a damp chilliness even on this warm August morning. He glared at the arrangement of white flowers in the sanctuary, disliking it even more than Browne did. It was dominated by cascades of the creamy white bells known for some reason as black dragon lilies. They looked better, Mitchell decided, with leaves on.

Browne turned to look at him and, realising that the small-talk was over and the interview under way, he hastily took out his notebook. Browne noted his glum expression and the uncharacteristic lack of efficiency and realised that he had not seen him on the home front for several days. Had he and Virginia fallen out? He discovered to his surprise that he rather hoped they hadn't. On the whole, he thought, they were good for each other.

He recalled himself to his interviewee. Morgan had the look of a leprechaun. It was basically in his features but he could have done something towards dispelling it by cutting shorter the tendrils that curled round his face and taking off the collarless, long-sleeved garment that Ginny or Zoe would have called a grandad shirt, or at least choosing it in a colour other than lilac. The eyes were as dark as the hair and, although Zoe's were blue, he saw it was from her father that she had inherited or learned her habit of eye-to-eye confrontation.

He turned, when requested, to give his personal details to Mitchell. 'Owen Glyn Morgan. That makes everyone expect me to be Welsh and musical.'

Browne thought he looked Jewish. The emaciated face had dark, strong features, full lips and luxuriant but tidily curling hair, making him look like an anorexic Barenboim.

'Instead,' Morgan continued, 'I was born and bred in Leeds and play the organ only because there was a vacancy here. I'm a compulsive volunteer. I can't bear that tense, fraught silence between help being asked and some plan being suggested to fill the need so I always fill it and this time it landed me with playing St Oswald's organ for the last two years. I've spent them trying to decide which is better, the monotonous but competent repetition of hymn tunes or proper organ pieces badly executed. I'm a compulsive talker too when I'm nervous.' But the compulsion, having been given its head, dried up and he sat in embarrassed silence regarding a point in the middle of Browne's chest.

Browne helped him out by patiently requesting an account of the weekend's activities from his witness's point of view. Mitchell filed away for his own further consideration the reflection that this question elicited more information about the people concerned in this case and their relations with one another than direct questioning on those lines would have done. Browne was given the facts about the choir practice that had become familiar to them both. Morgan reported, sympathetically, his daughter's difficulty with the minor third interval. 'It would have helped if Mrs Hunter hadn't waited with such obvious impatience for her children, wandering about from one of her flower arrangements to another till she got to the big white one. She knew then she was sufficiently in my sights in the organ mirror for an ostentatious consultation of her watch to be effective. I saw her clearly but I ignored her and took the four-part section over again. Then she came fussing over to tell me how she loved my anthem. I should have been flattered I suppose. Last time she talked to me she was telling me she loved Mozart, so I'm in good company. People who're sincere and not just trying to appear cultured usually mention a minor composer when they say they love somebody. You can't really say "I love Mozart". It's like saying "I love Mount Everest". It towers so far above other mountains in its challenge and reputation that people can't become familiar with it. It's there, like Mozart is, to be used as a measuring rod.'

Browne, who had always disliked his sergeant's wife, began to feel sorry for her in the face of this unanimous hostility towards her from all his witnesses whom she presumably thought of as her friends. Morgan perhaps caught something of his reflections.

'I'm sorry. I'm just annoyed with her for upsetting Zoe. She has enough problems trying to reconcile her frivolous teenage lifestyle with real musical ability and a fine voice. She's sometimes carried along by her enthusiasm but, mostly, she wishes to be rid of her talent to make getting along with her peers a bit simpler. She didn't want to sing the solo, especially as I'm choirmaster, and I was afraid she'd back out at the last minute.'

'She wouldn't have let you down.'

He looked surprised, then pleased. 'No, I don't think she would.' Enquiries about Saturday produced strictures on his brother. 'A first-rate show. He cast it well, then got the best out of the people he'd chosen. And he'd written it well to begin with. Pity he doesn't stick to that and leave preaching alone.'

'You prefer the line taken by Mr Priestley?'

'Good God, no! Rather Gerald than that. But he's so anxious to play the intellectual theologian. He reads Karl Barth and Don Cupitt and gets a religious vocabulary but not a religious experience. Then he jumbles it all up and produces a sermon out of it, like someone who opens three tins and claims he's cooked a meal. I'd rather grapple first hand with modern religious philosophers than hear him half explain what he's three-quarters understood.'

Mitchell, admiring his inspector's skill increasingly, noted down that the witness was enjoying his interview. Morgan had not joined the gathering for coffee in the Carrs' house and had been asleep in bed when his family returned.

They progressed to Sunday. 'Did you notice any activity out in the street before morning service?'

'Only the milkman, delivering a week's philosophy, a pretty accurate weather forecast and three pints of semi-skimmed. For reasons of his own he does a Sunday delivery and takes Monday off.'

'You didn't notice any of the Carr family moving around before they left for church?'

He shook his head. His account of the rest of the day denigrated Alan Priestley's sermon and commended his brother's cover drives and hook shots. He offered a version of the Carrs' marriage that was different from anything Browne had listened to so far. 'She couldn't be happy with anyone and blames everyone in the world for it but herself. He was a nice little bloke but not very perceptive. She's quite attractive now and at twenty-two she was a knockout. He probably married in haste and wondered what had hit him at leisure.'

Browne saved his last question till the organist, seeing Mitchell close his notebook, had relaxed. 'What had young Atkinson had to say to upset Carr on the night you had to rescue him from Poskitt's pub?'

'I've no idea. I was too busy attending to practical matters.' The answer came promptly but Morgan's knuckles whitened as he grasped the back of the pew.

* * *

106

Browne blinked as he emerged from the ecclesiastical dimness to the brightness outside. Only after several seconds was he able to focus on the gardens that demonstrated a conscientious effort on the part of the parishioners and perhaps the guidance of Mr Medway. The privet, however, had proved too much for them and bushy tufts of it provided the lower boundary of Browne's view of the moor where the cricket match had been played. Seeing the vicar closing his front door, he feared that parish business would delay the few words he'd intended to have with him but Garside beamed and came across to speak to him. 'I know I mustn't ask how the case is progressing so I'll just ask if there's anything else I can do for you.' He gestured towards the vicarage, an invitation to return there.

Browne shook his head and settled himself on the wooden bench facing a rose bed, diligently weeded, where Garside joined him. Mitchell squatted well within earshot on the daisy-sprigged grass. 'I thought you were setting off on some urgent mission,' Browne began.

Garside grinned. 'I am but a few minutes won't make any difference. The gales in the late spring brought the lightning conductor down. The nearest available steeplejacks are in Manchester or Nottingham and they'd charge a fortune just to come. Fortunately the local fire station has offered the use of its turntable ladder, so I was about to go up the tower to make a detailed examination of the damage to see whether I or an expert will have the privilege of adventuring in it to do the job. I'll take you up if you're interested and you can talk to me up there.'

Browne further reviewed his previous ideas about the nature of the clergy and noticed Mitchell's eager expression but he shook his head. 'Some other time when I'm not on duty, thanks all the same. I want some more information about Alan Priestley. More than one witness has suggested that he and Theresa Carr have been spending more time together than is wise. Any comment? Is he a straight homosexual or might he have some interest in her too?'

Garside sighed. 'My opinion, for what it's worth, is that neither of them has the least interest in the other except as fellow church members. There was an unfortunate incident a couple of weeks ago when Gary got himself into a temper because he thought Theresa was getting too involved in the festival weekend. He made various accusations concerning her and Alan and, in her distress,

Theresa explained why they could have no possible foundation. Gary threatened to tell me and various other people and have Alan generally discredited. He didn't do it as far as I know. He certainly didn't approach me. His rages were usually impotent and his threats, if ignored, were soon forgotten. Alan came to speak to me about it though and I believe he approached Theresa as well.'

Had he, Browne wondered, approached Gary Carr – and with more than arguments? 'You don't seem to find his aberration a serious obstacle spiritually.' Browne sounded surprised.

'Why should he?' demanded Mitchell from his station at their feet. 'Presumably he only chooses consenting adults to consort with. They can believe in God together can't they?'

Garside smiled. 'It rather mucks up His arrangements for the propagation of the species. But it is a serious spiritual obstacle to Alan, and not only because of the attitude of his fellow churchmen. His long-term partner died last year. His absence is less embarrassing for the congregation but it hasn't changed Alan's leanings. What worries me is that he needs to feel it's wrong. He enjoys his own guilt. His humiliation is a sort of stimulus to him.'

'I hear he has recently taken up with another partner.'

Garside replied carefully, 'I believe so.'

'I hear, too, that the new partner, Charles Atkinson, spent a riotous evening not very long ago with Gary Carr at the Rag and Louse.'

Garside nodded. 'I heard about it. It was then that he stopped coming to church. I've been meaning to go round to see what was wrong.'

He stopped speaking as his wife appeared at their front door. She caught sight of them and beckoned. Garside excused himself and hurried towards her. Browne and Mitchell followed him sufficiently closely to hear her tell him, 'Theresa's on the phone. Anne-Marie's disappeared and her bed hasn't been slept in.'

Chapter 11

Monica Kelly finished applying foundation to a remarkably well preserved complexion and wondered whether Dr Fenwick would call to see her during the morning. She peered into the dressing table mirror, rubbed in a smear on her chin and began applying lipstick. Satisfied after another minute with the effect she had achieved, she came through the curtain from the bedroom end of the long room and began patting the already plump and tidy cushions in her easy chairs.

A sharp ring of the doorbell produced a gratified smile which she replaced with an expression of long-suffering and a hand to her forehead as she went to let the doctor in. She was surprised when she saw that her visitor was her daughter. Theresa came past her, looking up the hall towards the sitting area, heedless of her mother's ungracious greeting. 'I didn't expect you'd be bothering with me this morning. Why aren't you at work?'

Theresa tried to disguise her dismay at not finding her own daughter ensconced in the deep armchair. 'I'm going in a bit later. I came here in case Anne-Marie had called. I forgot to give her a message before she left.'

'Was she coming here?'

'She didn't say so but I thought she might just call in passing to see how you were. You haven't seen her?'

'I haven't seen anybody. Everybody's far too busy getting on with their own lives to bother calling here. I don't suppose I'm down for a visit from Dr Fenwick today?'

Theresa sighed. 'I haven't seen his list. I told you I was going in later today.' She glanced at her mother impatiently. The old woman had obviously prepared herself. She was wearing the black dress which she knew emphasised her pallor and slight build, and had put on her 'brave little woman' make-up with the old-fashioned dark red lipstick which made her look ravaged yet not unattractive. Then her impatience suddenly evaporated as she noted the back, unwillingly bent to accommodate the unyielding cage of years, the expression a mixture of belligerence and appeal, wisdom and weakness, proficiency and dependence. Suddenly she felt a great pity for her mother's bewilderment at her physical limitations and the new conditions imposed by another generation that made her experience irrelevant and undervalued.

Mrs Kelly took the three steps necessary to reach the tiny kitchen. 'You'll want a cup of tea now you're here, I suppose.'

Theresa, breakfastless, anxious and needing a respite in which to replan her search for her daughter, accepted gratefully. As she busied herself about the kitchen, Mrs Kelly addressed Theresa through the door. 'I hope to goodness Mrs Grayson won't drop in again today. She moaned the whole of yesterday about that mongol grandson of hers. Who wants to listen to that morbid sort of talk? Anyway, it's her daughter-in-law who has to look after him, not her. I don't know how she'd manage if she had my problems to put up with. Her people are always here. She doesn't have a thing to do for herself. Some people are just lucky.'

She came back into the living room with a tray and deposited it on a table for Theresa to help herself. Then taking a fluffy yellow duster from the sideboard drawer, she removed a miscellany of small objects from the mantelpiece and proceeded to dust them and it vigorously. After a couple of minutes' self-righteous industry, she addressed Theresa over her shoulder. 'You shouldn't be letting me do this. Dr Fenwick said I was to get plenty of rest.'

Theresa put down her empty cup. 'I'm not making you do it.'

The dusting recommenced. 'You aren't volunteering either. It needs doing doesn't it? If you won't I'll have to.'

'I wouldn't say it needed doing.'

The old woman turned triumphantly. 'No, you wouldn't now! I knew he'd drag you down to his level. Anything did for him.'

Theresa sighed again and took the duster and her mother sat down smugly to drink her tea. 'Mrs Grayson was surprised that none of you came to see me yesterday. I made excuses for you as usual. She was asking me whether I'd be moving in with you now. It's a biggish house for just you, and the children won't be there for much longer – well, not Frank anyway. I told her you hadn't mentioned it and it wasn't my place to bring it up if you didn't.' She let the pause lengthen, suggestively.

Theresa banged the last trinket down on the mantelpiece. 'That would just suit you nicely, wouldn't it? Frank, who's the only one who ever resists you, away at university so you can brag about his achievements without having to put up with his company, and two women you can manipulate to do your bidding.'

Mrs Kelly stared in astonishment. 'I don't know what's got into you lately.'

Theresa perched on the chair arm and exulted in her new-found courage. 'Nothing has. It's been there all the time. It's just beginning to struggle to the surface and the struggle's going to be successful.'

Mrs Kelly found it safer to change the subject. 'I don't know what on earth you're talking about. I want you to take your father's gardening things for Frank.'

Theresa's anger was refuelled. 'You took them from old Mr Medway just to give them to Frank? He doesn't want them. He's not a keen gardener. He gives the old man a hand because he's good-natured and he does ours because it's a help to me.'

'Gary could have done it. He wasn't at work.'

'That's none of your affair, and no, I won't take the tools and things for Frank. You took them back just to be spiteful and you can get rid of them without my help.'

This failed to deflect Mrs Kelly from her late son-in-law's shortcomings. 'I can't think what made you marry him.'

'You did, Mother.'

Her astonishment was genuine. 'I did?'

'Yes, he asked me twice, and the only thing you'd ever taught me to do was obey, be agreeable. I was terrified of offending, refusing. And I'm not sorry. We had some happy times. You wouldn't think so, but then, I never wanted to be your sort of wife. You wanted life velvet lined, flower scented. You behaved for your whole married life like a spoilt child. Not only could Father not share his worries with you, he had to pretend he hadn't any. If something hadn't happened in your front room, it was of no interest to you. You switched the world news off the television and watched moronic quiz games because you "liked to see the prizes". You imagined all those showy gadgets and gimmicks installed in your house for all your relations and neighbours to admire and

111

envy and you reproached Father because he couldn't rush out and get them all for you. You even had rules for what he could talk about. He hadn't to introduce a topic that you were unqualified to pronounce on, so all we talked about was what other people had and what we planned to get. Anyone who introduced topics of general interest was accused of showing off or trying to cut you out.'

Theresa was trembling and out of breath but Mrs Kelly was rallying. She rose with dignity. 'If you're going to talk to me like that, I wish you hadn't come.'

The stand against her mother had released all the tension in Theresa. She could think clearly. She would go home and ring the vicarage and if Philip had no news of Anne-Marie, she would contact the police. 'That makes two of us,' she told her mother. She rose to leave, glancing through the window. 'You've got another visitor. It's Sergeant Hunter.'

'Is that the tall, thin, blond one who goes to your church? He seems a nice man.'

Theresa was at the front door. 'Yes, by your definition, he probably is.'

Hunter, with Bellamy in his wake, had been regarding with approval the modern, functional building with its rows of flat windows and low tiled roof that housed the district's old people. It looked honest and useful, easy of access and economical to heat. The windows and doors were aluminium framed and double glazed and tubs with flowering shrubs stood by the main door. The garden consisted of large and small colourful flower beds that would require minimum maintenance. A small porch jutted out from the main building, its woodwork painted a sensible burgundy. The yellowish brick looked faintly antiseptic against the dirty sandstone of the Congregational church next door, the rival or sister of St Oswald's according to your viewpoint, with its imitation Perpendicular windows and huge, steeply pitched roof. Decorative fencing tactfully hid dustbins and over that he could see a tall privet hedge and an end-on view of the row of three-storey houses that ran up to St Oswald's at the top of the hill. The whole panorama was framed by and dotted with trees.

The morning sun was beating down on their heads and Hunter was tempted to steal a few minutes' rest on one of the high-backed rustic benches in the shade of the building. They faced a bed of roses which surrounded a weeping cherry, weeping at the moment only slightly pink-tinted leaves. Then he had made determinedly for the door. This was, after all, only the second witness he'd been allowed to interrogate in this case.

Mrs Kelly was less than pleased to see them. She had been shaken by her daughter's first rebellion and thwarted too. Theresa had been allowed to escape before just retribution had been exacted. After inviting the two officers inside and seating them she sank into an easy chair herself with a weariness that was not feigned.

Hunter wasted no time on pleasantries. 'We weren't able to ask all the questions we needed to whilst you were in hospital so we wanted to see you again. I hope you're feeling better now.'

'I suppose I'm as right as I'm going to be,' she allowed, grudgingly. 'What do you want to know?'

'First of all, the time you rang your daughter on July the thirty-first, the Tuesday when Mr Carr was last seen alive.'

She put a hand to her head. 'I can't remember exact times nowadays. Besides, I wasn't very well. I'm still not well.'

'You surprise me,' Hunter told her deviously. 'You strike me as the sort of person who is always observant, even when their own indisposition might excuse them from noticing what's going on.'

'I suppose I am.' Her attention was caught now and she warmed further towards this young man whose refined appearance had always predisposed her to approve of him. 'It must have been about nine. I could make you a pot of tea if you like.'

At a signal from Hunter, Bellamy, who was longing for ice cold lager, expressed their deep appreciation. She put the kettle on and went through to collect the milk from the front door. Finding only the empty bottles she had put out, her expression darkened. 'Not there of course.' She stood in the kitchen doorway and chuntered at them. 'He goes early to all the big houses in his round. They're the ones he makes his packet out of. Never thinks of all the money he's had out of us in the past. We don't matter now. Money talks. I wanted some cream a week or two ago. Left a note out the day before and he comes with some story about having a short delivery himself. You can believe that if you like!' she told him with heavy sarcasm.

'What did your daughter say?' Hunter cut in. She blinked at

113

him. 'When you rang her on Tuesday?' She still looked blank. It was a leading question but he had no option. 'Did she tell you that they were packing for your son-in-law to go to Harlow?'

She shook her head. 'No, she didn't tell me that, but then, she never tells me anything. She's never here to tell me anything.'

'She wouldn't want to burden you with her affairs when she was worried about you,' Hunter soothed.

She nodded, half mollified. 'Anyway, the less said about him the better.' Hunter's familiarity with elderly witnesses told him that this was merely the prologue to extensive comment. 'She wouldn't have had to work if he'd done as he should by her. Always reckoned there wasn't work to be had in his line. Such nonsense. How does Frank find it then? That Bradford business was right up his street. Redundancy, life of idleness, grounds for thinking life had treated him shabbily. What more could a man like him want? If he was made redundant, that is. I wouldn't be surprised if he just got the sack.'

'How long did your daughter take to arrive?'

'Hardly any time at all. I will say that for her.'

Hunter looked up, quickly. 'Didn't the car play her up?'

'She didn't tell me that. She was very quick.' The kettle whistled but she had forgotten the tea and merely switched it off. 'Now, what was I telling you? Oh yes, he had this story about getting a short delivery. I noticed Mrs Grayson got her tub though before he ran out. Or that's what he said. Just because she orders two pints a day. It's all very well for her. I'd have got two pints myself if there were any call for it but I don't get the visitors she gets.'

'What happened between Theresa arriving and Dr Fenwick being summoned?' Hunter asked, desperately.

She cast her mind back and then answered slowly, like a child rehearsing a lesson, 'Theresa made some tea and then she got me to bed. Then she went outside. I expect it was because of the car if it was broken.'

'Didn't you wonder what they were doing?'

'I always wonder what they're doing. They're never here looking after me.'

'And you were feeling much worse when they came in?'

'No, as a matter of fact, I felt a bit better, no thanks to them.'

'But they decided to send for the doctor?'

114

'Well, I suppose once they'd got their precious car sorted out they had time to notice me. Lucky I didn't die while they were outside. Anyway, Dr Fenwick soon realised it was serious.' Her voice rose importantly. 'He made sure Theresa came to see me on Sunday. He brought her himself. I don't suppose she'd have bothered otherwise. He's a queer young man for a doctor, spiky hair and odd clothes, very modern but always extremely good quality. The other patients were quite impressed that my doctor came to see me as a visitor but I told them, he knows what's due. He's quite interested in Theresa, though she's older of course. She'd have had her chances with him if only she'd waited. Not that he's been to see me much since. Theresa says I can ring if I need him, but he ought to take a bit of interest, show some concern.'

'Your daughter accompanied you in the ambulance didn't she?'

'That's right and Frank came chasing after us with the car so she wouldn't have to walk or catch a bus when she'd got me safely stowed away. What a piece of cake her life is.'

'Make your mind up,' muttered Bellamy under his breath. 'I thought she'd worked herself to a shadow to support her husband.'

'No one drove me around in cars,' Mrs Kelly went on relentlessly, 'when I visited my mother I had to walk up the street under my own steam. Now, what was I telling you? Oh yes, Mrs Grayson's visitors. Her people are always here. She doesn't have to do anything for herself. Some people have all the luck. She was surprised that none of the family came to see me yesterday. I made excuses for them as usual. She was wondering why I don't move in with Theresa and the children. I had to pretend I prefer it here. It's a big house for just her and Frank won't be around for much longer but of course it's not my place to bring it up if she doesn't. Of course Frank's spoilt. He's allowed to say whatever he likes. Dresses like a tramp too. Not like that nice clean-looking boy you've brought with you.'

Bellamy blushed and squirmed but Hunter ignored his discomfiture. He was still hoping that this stream of self-pity and resentment, if unchecked, would inadvertently reveal something useful. 'My wife saw Anne-Marie at her Confirmation class last

115

night,' he told Mrs Kelly. 'She said she and her friend Paula would be coming to see you today.'

The old woman looked anxious rather than pleased. 'I don't want Anne-Marie bringing her here. I don't want Anne-Marie seeing her at all. Tell her to bring Zoe to see me.' She refused steadfastly to give any reason for her disapproval of Paula or her new attitude to Zoe.

Chapter 12

Hunter arrived back at the station to the welcome news that his chief inspector was waiting for him at the Rag and Louse. Visions of prawn salad and a foaming pint lent wings to his feet as he made for the car park instead of the cobbled street that led to the Fleece. If Browne was abandoning the station local in favour of Poskitt's place it must be a working lunch. Leaving his car in the pub park, he went straight through the dim, low-ceilinged building and emerged into a flagged yard where a customer informed him Browne had appropriated a table. He found him in the shadow of a huge blue-and-yellow-striped umbrella, absorbed in the contents of a small red book.

'What's the beer like here?'

Browne looked up. 'Haven't tried it. I wanted to ask Poskitt if he had any idea why Carr got drunk in Charles Atkinson's company.'

'Because he was being treated?'

'Possibly.'

'What were you reading?'

'Fairy stories I hope. In some ways that would mean more problems for the people concerned but it would be less work for us.'

'You'd better read me one.' He sank on to a white plastic chair as Browne obliged.

' "Daddy came to my room again tonight. He had nothing on under his dressing gown. He said he was cold and wasn't I going to invite him into my warm bed. I didn't dare not to. He put his dressing gown on the bed as an extra cover. It was brown and orange and it didn't go with my pink sheets. His hands were cold when he started to stroke me. Then he began doing things that are too horrible to write about . . ." '

Hunter blinked. 'Are there any more stories in that book?'

'Plenty. How about this one? "I took Paula into the park this afternoon. She thought we were going on the swings but I wanted to give her a good talking to. I know she's still glue-sniffing with that crowd that meets in the junior school yard at night. I can tell by those sores round her mouth . . ." '

'I think I need a drink and some lunch before I hear any more.'

Browne shook his head. 'I told Poskitt to bring pints and beef sandwiches as soon as he saw you come through. Listen to just one more, then we can talk as we eat and afterwards you can borrow this little volume and browse in it yourself.'

The laden barman appeared on cue, and Hunter drank and nibbled a sandwich, having bidden a reluctant farewell to his hoped-for prawns. When they had the yard to themselves again, Browne continued reading.

' "I read an interesting story this week about a girl called Josephine who poisoned her grandad because he wouldn't let her go to ballet lessons. She was younger than me and Daddy deserves much worse than the grandfather. He might have given me AIDS. It would be a way out of my problem. If I decide to do it I couldn't manage it all on my own but I expect I could get Frank to help me." '

Browne put the diary down and, in three huge bites, disposed of his first sandwich. Hunter had taken his to pieces and was carefully removing a frill of fat from each pink slice of meat. 'I don't need to ask whose but why have we got it?'

'She's apparently done a runner. Not seen since she said she was going to bed last night. When she didn't come down to breakfast her mother discovered her bed hadn't been slept in.'

Browne pictured again the pink and white frilly room, painfully neat in contrast with the casual untidiness of the rest of the house. Just the reverse of the Morgans next door. He had arrived expecting to find Theresa calmly coping as usual and had found her in floods of tears. He hadn't yet decided whether the loss, even temporarily, of her daughter affected her more than the permanent loss of her husband or whether Anne-Marie's disappearance was the last straw or, indeed, whether there was some other reason for her unnatural control to have snapped just now. She had sat on her daughter's bed and sobbed quietly as Browne made his meticulous search, her dismay increasing when the diary was found in a drawer containing underclothes. 'She always keeps it in the drawer of her bedside table. I looked for it there!' Theresa had exclaimed involuntarily.

'So that you could remove it before I arrived?' he had asked and she had nodded ruefully.

'Did she have any idea what was in it?' Hunter had reassembled his sandwich but was nibbling it as suspiciously as before.

Browne shrugged. 'She insisted she hadn't read it. I think I believe her. It's probably a point of honour with her to allow her children the privacy she was denied. She probably suspects it will make pretty weird reading but she might not have much more idea than we have whether any particular part of it is true unless it directly concerns herself. There's another bit where she says – Anne-Marie I mean – that she tried to persuade her mother to show someone the bruises she'd sustained when Carr hit her. From all we've heard of Carr, physical violence doesn't seem in character but we might have a word with Fenwick and the vicar about it.'

'Isn't it more important to discover whether Carr sexually abused his daughter?'

'Not really, now he's dead. Well, not for us anyway. What is important is finding whether Mrs Carr or Frank believed it. I've thought up to now that, although on paper she's our most likely suspect, she really was trying to make a go of her marriage, but if she'd recently got an inkling of this we'd have to think again.'

Hunter pushed his plate aside, abandoning the remains of his sandwich. 'Could Anne-Marie be responsible for the poisoning itself? She wouldn't have had to remove or burn the body. Her mother or Frank or even Morgan could have helped and shielded her.'

'Morgan? To make less trouble for Mrs Carr you mean? Or because she claimed to be clearing the way for him with her mother?' Browne shook his head in bewilderment. 'I wish we had a more exact time of death. The child's vouched for during the greater part of Tuesday evening. She arrived at her Confirmation class at seven thirty and Carr didn't leave the pub till after eight. She was with the vicar till he delivered her to the Morgans' house and God knows where her father was by then. Jennie Smith's report says Garside didn't watch her into the house but he left her at five to ten and Christine Morgan says she arrived at about

119

ten. She was there or at home with her family till they all went to bed. They can vouch for each other. Trouble is, they could all be in it together. And if he was poisoned I suppose it could have been in something that was left for him to eat after our customer had gone out.'

Hunter drained his glass. 'I suppose we're assuming that both the diary and the disappearing act are just attention-seeking ploys but what if something nasty's happened to the kid?'

'Don't worry. Everything's been set in motion. I'm not taking any chances. There's another thing. Have a look at the passages I've marked.' Thin slips of paper indicated where Hunter was to read. 'I'd guess that a lot of that stuff is quotation. All the references to AIDS and glue-sniffing tabulate the facts so neatly that I get the impression she's got it all from leaflets picked up in Fenwick's surgery when she's been waiting for her mother to finish work. And when she's writing about what her father's supposed to have done to her, there's a drawing of the veil at just the point where an emotive article on child abuse in a magazine would stop giving details.'

'That's all right then.'

'I'm not sure that it is. The passage about poisoning is dated just a week before Carr was killed. Even if all this stuff is fantasy, she seems to fill in the days in the right order. And the bit about the colour of her father's dressing gown clashing with the colour of her sheet rings true. It's not the sort of detail she'd put in if she hadn't seen it. Want another?'

Hunter shook his head. 'Only coffee and we'd better have that back at work. It's well into the afternoon.'

Sending Hunter on to see to it, Browne paused in the now almost empty bar to put his question to the landlord.

Poskitt considered. 'Aye, it were t'young lad as 'ad 'is 'and in 'is pocket. Not that Carr 'ad much more'n a couple o'pints, mind. It were because 'e weren't used to it.'

'And the elder Mr Morgan took him home?'

'Aye, though there weren't no call for it. He were talkin' a load o' rubbish but it weren't offensive like.'

'Can you remember anything he said?'

Poskitt scratched his chin. 'Well, not word fer word of course. 'E were boastin' about 'is lad but 'e were reckonin' 'e'd already been to t'university and got 'is degree.'

'And Mr Morgan took him home to stop him making a fool of himself – being a good neighbour?'

'Oh, Glyn were a bit more than that. They were old mates, went to school together.' He grinned. 'They were allus on about the tricks they got up to there. They 'ad some boring old English master. Wakeham 'e were called an' 'is initial was "I". "I. Wakeham".' He guffawed. 'That's what 'e 'ad ter do when 'e'd sent 'em ter sleep. One day . . .' Browne raised a hand to stem the flow.

'You don't know what Mr Atkinson and Mr Carr were talking about?'

''Fraid not. I was busy and they were both 'uddled in that far corner.'

Browne thanked the landlord and departed. Back in his office he drank his coffee in silence as he went through the latest batch of reports. He had read them through by the time Hunter came in. 'Dean's still interviewing the Carrs' neighbours. He hasn't unearthed any more useful information but he's made the negative point that not only did no one see Carr leave home a second time but no one saw him return beforehand. Yet several folk saw him leave for the pub in the early evening. What if he didn't go back home? Where else might he have gone? And Dean's been back to the Rag and Louse. Poskitt was very busy when he took that phone call for Carr, but thinking back he says perhaps it wasn't Mrs Carr's voice who asked for him.'

'Have we found out who Carr spoke to in the pub car park?' Hunter asked, reaching for an upright chair and sitting astride it backwards. He leaned to the left to close the door, misjudged the angle and was deposited in a heap at Browne's feet.

'Walter Crossley was the only one of the crowd the barmaid could name. Bellamy's going to talk to him after he's done with Atkinson. If you've quite finished the gymnastics display, perhaps you can tell me how you got on this morning.'

Hunter settled himself. 'I saw Fenwick briefly. He confirmed Mrs Carr's account from about ten o'clock on the thirty-first.'

'We'll have to see him again now on several counts. What about Mrs Kelly?'

Hunter described his visit in detail. 'I know she's a bit economical with the truth, sir, but there were some quite marked variations from the story we've heard from the rest of the Carrs. She wasn't told Gary was going away, but I suppose that's not important. It's interesting that she gave Theresa credit for arriving quickly. Theresa told us she took much longer than usual. Her mother's impatient enough. She'd be likely to complain if she'd been kept waiting. What was oddest of all was that Mrs Kelly claimed to be recovering by the time the doctor was summoned and yet she was still ill enough to be sent to hospital. What was more important than dealing with an old woman's serious illness when they first arrived? Mind you, we'd better ask Fenwick about her condition before we draw any silly conclusions. The old lady will tell any story that suits her own purpose. She says Fenwick accompanied Theresa to the hospital on Sunday night. She took it as a mark of respect for herself but she did suggest that he was interested in Theresa. Of course she works for him and she wasn't well herself. Fenwick was very likely just being ordinarily considerate. Still, we'd better not rule out some relationship there.'

'Right. Anything else?'

Hunter recounted Mrs Kelly's objections to her granddaughter's friend. 'Isn't there something in the diary about her? If Mrs Kelly's heard about it, perhaps there's some truth in that bit at least.'

Browne rang for more coffee. 'I'll tell you what I've picked up from the Morgans whilst we drink this.' He gave a succinct account of the three interviews. 'That was a cute question of Mitchell's. I think we know now where the body was between the Tuesday and the Saturday. I'll get the boot of the Carrs' Mini gone over by forensic but if the body was wrapped carefully in a huge polythene wheelchair bag we aren't likely to find very much. The car Zoe heard on the Saturday night was probably either Theresa or Frank or more likely both taking the remains to the spinney. That must have been what the railway guard heard too. The time's right. All we need now is some proof. Anne-Marie told Zoe that there'd been an affair between Carr and another woman but she didn't believe her.'

Hunter shook his head. 'He wasn't the type. I'm not sure about Theresa. Anne-Marie's suggestions about Priestley are nonsense, of course, but I don't know about Morgan.'

Browne stood up. 'I've made an appointment for us. Never mind what I said earlier, I'd like you with me when I speak to Priestley so get a car and we'll be off. I'll drop you at Fenwick's surgery when we've finished and you can tidy up various points with him. I shall come back here. Master Frank was conveniently missing again this morning, cycling around asking his sister's friends if they'd seen her. Plausible enough except that he's never yet been available when we've wanted him. I've left a message that he's to report to the station at five. Thank goodness he's seventeen. We'll see if we as well as Mr Watmough can't get him to show us the whites of his eyes.'

Chapter 13

'Tell me,' Browne commanded, as Hunter turned the car into the street of tiny, well-cared-for terraced houses which was his destination, 'what you've managed to find out about young Atkinson.'

'Not a lot. More or less what Bellamy picked up from interviewing him.'

'When we've put Priestley through the hoop I'll leave you to grill young Atkinson. You've got a free hand so long as you find out what he was up to on Tuesday the thirty-first.'

Hunter drew up behind Priestley's van. 'He's a young chap just down from some university.'

'Nottingham,' put in Browne.

'He's come to work in town somewhere for the summer.'

'Garden centre in Winding Lane,' supplied Browne helpfully. 'According to him he decided to befriend and treat Carr because he felt sorry for him. Some of the regulars were giving him a bit of stick.'

Hunter acknowledged the gratuitous information. 'Started coming to St Oswald's about two months ago. He had digs that he didn't much like and Alan let him move in here when he discovered that he was – well, like himself.'

Hunter's face was averted but Browne watched impatiently as the back of the sergeant's neck crimsoned and when he spoke his voice was sharp. 'The day you learn to call a spade a spade, Jerry, is when you'll begin getting a great deal more out of your witnesses and getting on a great deal better with your colleagues. For goodness' sake try to speak the language of the people once in a while and forget the elocution lessons you had from your maiden aunt.'

'Sir.' Flushing a deep red, Hunter came round to open the

passenger door for him with exaggerated politeness. Browne was distracted from wondering if he had made things worse by the side-on view of Priestley's van. Inscribed on it in primary colours was what seemed to him approximately half of the New Testament. The other half, he discovered, as he turned towards the house, had been reserved for stickers in the front window. Alan Priestley, when he appeared, prompt on the first peal of his bell, had the final couple of sentences on badges on his lapel. His face with its slack jaw had an unfinished look, as though its creator had been interrupted. There was a homespun quality about him, so that his body as well as his sweater seemed to have been hand-knitted. The effect was emphasised by a shaggy, unprofessional looking haircut which he had tried to brush back tidily. Browne had met too many homosexuals to think he could recognise one. What he did recognise, thanks to summer holidays in his childhood spent with his Pentecostal grandmother, was the portion of scripture on one of the badges and the way to ingratiate himself with this witness.

'John, chapter three, verse sixteen,' was his greeting to Mr Priestley and he was home and dry. His arms were grasped as Priestley drew him, beaming, into the miniature sitting room. 'You're welcome, brother.' Hunter strove to conceal his amusement.

Both officers were astonished to find all the available seats occupied by seven large, middle-aged ladies whose beams of welcome matched their host's. A buxom rump was edged more firmly into the corner of the settee to vacate a small strip of cushion, towards which Priestley waved Hunter as he busily unfolded a garish canvas garden chair which had been leaning against the wall. When Browne was safely ensconced in it he went back to stand beside a small table from where he had obviously been officiating when their ring had disturbed him. On it lay a large Bible, opened, and several sheets of closely written notes.

Hunter shot an anguished glance at his chief inspector, but for the moment it both amused and suited Browne to let matters proceed. He found they were being addressed and the theme of the meeting was explained to them. '. . . the Lord's dealing with our departed brother having guided our thoughts to what Scripture says about the destructive yet refining qualities of fire.' The ladies nodded as one, some of them murmuring inarticulate agreement.

'David the psalmist beseeches the Lord, "In the day when I call, answer me speedily. For my days are consumed like smoke and my bones are burned as an hearth." ' Browne reflected that if the Lord had done such a wholesale job on Gary Carr, his own task would have been considerably more difficult.

'And again He says, "The earth opened and swallowed up Dathan and covered the company of Abiram. And a fire was kindled in their company. The flame burned up the wicked." ' Priestley's eyes were closed and these verses quoted with no reference to the sheaf of notes. He certainly knew his stuff. ' "Through the wrath of the Lord of Hosts," says the prophet Isaiah, "is the land darkened, and the people shall be as the fuel of the fire; no man shall spare his brother." ' Browne thought this was rather near the bone but the ladies were unperturbed and the enthusiastic murmurs continued. 'And in the Revelation of St John we read, "the fourth angel poured out his vial upon the sun and power was given unto him to scorch men with fire. And men were scorched with great heat and blasphemed the name of God." '

It occurred to Browne that Priestley's thoughts had been guided by means of a concordance, but then, why not? The torrent of references rolled on. 'And the writer of Proverbs asks us, "Can a man take fire in his bosom and his clothes not be burned? Can one go upon hot coals and his feet not be burned?" ' Gary Carr's weren't, fortunately for himself and his team.

Now, apparently, the meeting had been thrown open for general contributions. The ladies offered their thoughts and feelings in a waterfall of mixed metaphor, each of them catching up the basic theme and embroidering on it. Just as Browne was vowing never again to arrive early for an interview, Priestley suggested that the proceedings be brought to a close with a hymn, so that his brother could do the worldly work that, by God's leading, had brought him into their midst. Avoiding Hunter's eye, Browne rose with the ladies, accepted the tattered sheet of choruses that was thrust into his hand and gave vent to an enthusiastic rendering of 'Burn, Fire, burn', the tune of which, from its predictability, he picked up after a couple of lines. Once through proved not sufficient and the company rapidly became drunk on the repeated melody. He shuddered at the reduction of a profound truth to this childish jingle to which the lady beside him responded with clapping and foot tapping. He suspected that her satisfaction had its source in

126

the regular rhythm rather than any import that remained in the banal words.

He became aware, suddenly, of Hunter's strong tenor elaborating the four bar theme in true jazz fashion. Their eyes met and Browne received the message that he had got them into this and he could get them out of it. They both stopped singing and, possibly taking the hint, the ladies made this repetition the final one. Their hands were shaken enthusiastically by each departing attender. 'There's One knows better than we do,' declared the last one, firmly but ambiguously. Browne wondered whether One had ever dared to disagree with her. Nevertheless, the company had neither offended nor embarrassed him. He had found a dignity in their utter sincerity that he had to respect. He began to understand something of what Philip Garside had tried to explain.

He was impatient now to be about his business and he accepted Priestley's offer of tea only on condition that he could sit in the kitchen and question him while he made it. Priestley had remained at home on July 31st with only his guest, Charles Atkinson, for company. 'I expect you know by now about my problem so you probably won't accept him as an alibi,' he added defiantly.

Browne sighed. 'We're aware that you're a homosexual. If it doesn't worry the vicar overly, it certainly isn't our concern, provided that the young man I saw disappearing out of the kitchen is of an appropriate age.'

Averting his gaze, Priestley muttered, 'He's twenty-two.'

He spoke about his 'problem' as though it were epilepsy or diabetes, Browne thought. He supposed in a way it was like that. It was more inborn than overeating or alcoholism. He remembered reading somewhere that four per cent of men are truly homosexual and the cause was attributed to having a weak father and a mother who ruled the home. But then, he'd read somewhere else that it resulted from a feeling of rejection because a child of the opposite sex had been desired.

Another dilemma was concerning Priestley as he poured the promised tea. 'Maybe Charles would be less tempted somewhere else?' Without waiting for a reaction to this, he passed Hunter's cup with another question. 'Do you think I should give up the Lord's work until I have conquered my – er – ?'

'Problem?' supplied Hunter. Sarcastically? Helpfully? Browne sat back to see how Hunter would answer. 'We all have besetting sins,' his sergeant volunteered. 'I wasn't sure about yours until all this business blew up. I've heard you preach many a sermon that told me something I hadn't realised about myself. I don't think any of them were less valuable because you're a – er – homosexual.'

Priestley fixed his eyes on Hunter earnestly. 'Do you resent not having known? The Epistles have so much to say about confessing our sins one to another but Mr Garside always said it wouldn't be edifying to the congregation. No one else has my particular cross to bear so he doesn't think I'm failing others by not speaking about it in public.' He seemed almost proud of the exclusive nature of his aberration.

'The church's attitude to the question has altered drastically in the last few years,' Hunter put in.

The remark was a mistake. Priestley took Browne's arm and transferred his anxious gaze from Hunter to include him. 'But God's Word hasn't. St Paul writes to the Romans of "men with men, working that which is unseemly" and the rules laid down in Leviticus don't make an exception of me. "If a man lie with mankind as he lieth with a woman, both of them have committed an abomination." '

This was not what Browne had come for. 'In a few minutes I should like to speak to Mr Atkinson, whose veracity I shall not judge by his sexual habits. In the meantime, perhaps you could describe your movements on Saturday, August the fourth.' His tone of voice caused Hunter to take out his notebook and Priestley to resume his seat.

'Charles and I attended the pageant. It was very well produced but I'm not sure it was edifying to the young people who were acting in it.'

'Did you stay to the end?' Browne continued inexorably.

Priestley nodded. 'I sat between Charles and old Mr Medway. I fetched the old man's coffee and biscuits for him when it was over.'

'And then?'

'Charles and I walked home, bathed and had an early night.'

'Did either of you leave the house again before going to church on Sunday morning?'

He shook his head and blinked. 'Unless you count the garden.

128

I spent half an hour out there after breakfast, preparing myself for the morning service.'

'In sight of the house?'

'Probably not. I was down among the bushes at the end. Anyway, Charles doesn't get up early on Sundays so he wouldn't have seen me after I got up at eight o'clock.'

He stopped as he saw Hunter and Browne exchange glances. 'I thought,' Hunter remarked, 'that you and Mr Atkinson became friendly because you both attended St Oswald's.'

Priestley bit his lip. 'You're right. That's where we met. He attended regularly at first and took a great interest in everybody. He became quite friendly with the Morgans and they invited him to tea one Sunday. He came back here afterwards and wouldn't go to church and he hasn't been since. He's obviously got some sort of problem but I know better than to interfere until he's ready to open up about it. He's just the same as ever with me.'

'If we could return to Sunday morning,' Browne put in.

'Oh, yes, I had a cup of tea just before half-past nine and left soon afterwards. I was walking in the spinney by quarter to ten.'

'Did you go to church by car?' Priestley nodded. 'And what time did you find the body in the spinney?'

'About ten.'

'How do we know that that isn't when you took Gary Carr's body from the boot of your car and dumped it there?' Priestley stared at Browne, eyes glazed. 'You went to see Mrs Carr because you were afraid her husband was about to damage your reputation with the education authority. That seems a very good motive to me.'

'But he wasn't going to. Theresa said she had known him and he had had no intention of ruining my good name.' He stopped, hearing her words over again and the significance of the tense she had used sank in. He hurried on, hoping to distract his interrogator from the same realisation. 'At first, Gary thought I was trying to win his wife's affections from him.' Browne smiled to himself at the old-fashioned expression. 'That wasn't true either. Theresa was much fonder of her husband than he deserved. She had no interest of that kind in either me or Gerald.'

Browne nodded. 'So you think Mrs Carr knew that her husband was dead when you went to see her?'

129

Priestley's expression was truculent. 'I think no such thing. I think poor Theresa may have thought her marriage was over and that Gary wouldn't come back to her again. And you don't really think I had a body in my car or you'd have had it in long ago for your people to examine.'

'We're about ready to rectify that omission now. Perverting the course of justice in favour of a homosexual partner would be a very serious matter too.'

Browne could not decide whether the shock Priestley's face registered was caused by fear, indignation or puzzlement. Before it wore off and to pre-empt protestations he took a sheaf of photographs from his jacket pocket. 'I'd be grateful if you'd take a look at these shots taken after Zoe had found the body and tell me if they differ in any way from what you noticed when you saw it earlier.'

Priestley peered at them, then excused himself to fetch his reading glasses from the room where the meeting had been held. He came back wearing them and gave the pictures his close attention. When he looked up his expression was anxious. 'I'm sure when I saw the body earlier on it wasn't half covered with all those leaves. I remember because I wondered whether to cover it up myself in the hope that no one would notice it till the services were over but I thought I'd be in trouble with your good selves if I changed anything so I left it alone.'

'Well, thanks for that much at least. Anything else?'

'I don't think so. I didn't hang around. I went back to head off anyone who might have had the same idea as me of spending a few minutes' meditation in such otherwise pleasant surroundings. It was a good job I did. I met young Frank hurrying up the track but I turned him back. I told him it was getting near service time and asked him about his cricket team. He walked back to church with me and I left him getting a lecture from his sister for rushing off and leaving her wondering where he was.'

'Might he have gone back to the spinney after you went into the vestry?'

'Ah, you think he'd arranged to meet young Zoe up there? No, he wouldn't have had time. It really was time for morning service and he was there from the beginning, sitting beside Mr Medway and finding the places for him in the prayer book. He's getting very arthritic these days and his fingers fumble the pages. Frank's

130

very good to him. Helps him in the garden too. Look, why do you think Charles has anything to do with this?'

He was distracted again, this time by a rapping on the kitchen door. 'That'll be my young neighbour. She's helping me to sow some biennials for planting out next spring – at least, she thinks she's helping me. Her mother only came home from hospital last week with her new twins so I try to amuse Samantha sometimes whilst she's busy with the babies.' He paused on his way to let her in. 'I can't think why you're dragging Charles into it.'

The door was opened to reveal a blonde child, runny-nosed, staggering under the weight of a large tray. 'I got 'em all out for you, Uncle Alan,' she announced proudly. She had indeed. The colourful packets had all been torn open and the contents inextricably mixed together in a pile against the wooden rim. Browne judged it time to go. Leaving Hunter to speak to Mr Atkinson, he thanked Priestley for his help. Priestley hovered behind him as he made for the front door. As he raised his hand in a farewell salute, Browne was visited by another felicitous flashback to his evangelical grandmother. ' "My brethren," ' he announced to his fuming companion, ' "count it all joy when ye fall into diverse temptations." James, one, verses two and three.' Wearing a rueful expression, Priestley closed his door quietly. ' "Knowing this," ' continued Browne to himself, as he leaned against his car and shook with mirth, ' "that the trying of your faith worketh patience." '

But when he had settled himself into the driver's seat, he found Priestley had had the last word. Slipping the photographs he had shown him into an inside pocket, he found, sticking out from amongst them, a slip of paper with familiar red and black printing. 'Seek ye first,' it advised him, 'the Kingdom of God and all these things shall be added unto you.'

131

Chapter 14

Hunter thought that the exterior of Fenwick's surgery, with ivy on one wall and evergreen shrubs in brick troughs, must look pretty much the same summer and winter. Behind a car park of intricately arranged cement blocks stood a one-storey building of red brick with long, narrow, black-framed windows. Red doors inside the porch tried to be cheerful but in the burning sun their glow was almost menacing. They were decorated with brass plates etched with several names, each with its imposing and mysterious following of abbreviated qualifications, probably meant to instil confidence but often, Hunter imagined, inspiring awe if not fear.

The industrious patterning of the car park continued in the building. The crested ridge tiles, reminding him of the edging on a paper doiley, topped a roof of conventional tiling. The corners of the building and the arch over the door featured stone facings in a pattern of battlements. Wooden slats in the sides of the porch were carefully arranged in rows at forty-five degrees to the ground.

The scene did not soothe Hunter as he trudged along the path to the door and before going inside he let his eyes rest gratefully on the calming greyish brown of the stone hospital annexe in the background. He had expected when they first set out that Browne would drop him off at the surgery rather than leaving him behind to interview the effete Charles Atkinson. He had had to walk the baking three-quarters of a mile from Priestley's house at a cracking pace so as not to keep Fenwick waiting too long at the end of his afternoon surgery.

Hunter considered Browne's recently uttered accusation. Could it have been Priestley's car that dumped the body on the night of August 5th? He could see that, in Browne's book, protecting his lover was a more credable reason for failing to report the discovery of a body than the one Priestley had given. Hunter, who knew the man better, could well believe he had acted from either motive. There was obviously some connection between Atkinson and the Carrs that would bear further investigation.

He wiped his face with a spotless handkerchief and wished he were the sort of man who felt comfortable working in casual dress and jacketless. Mitchell was probably pursuing his house-to-house enquiry in shorts and a vest! Atkinson had merely agreed with everything Priestley had said. After all, they'd had long enough to rehearse it together. He had taken a seemingly interminable time to repeat it all. Recalling himself to his present situation, Hunter hoped that if Fenwick had been kept waiting it had not made him less cooperative or willing to divulge useful information.

He was dismayed as he went in to see the waiting room almost half full. Two receptionists were busy behind the counter by the door but there was no sign of Theresa Carr. The younger of the two smiled at him as he introduced himself. 'You've a long wait, I'm afraid, unless you interrupt his schedule. The majority of these people are waiting to see Dr Fenwick. He chats to them all and takes an interest in their families and every appointment overruns its five minutes so he gets further and further behind as the surgery goes on.'

Hunter sighed. If Fenwick gave so much attention to his patients at least he would know something about them. He sat down resignedly. Waiting for anything is a depressing pastime and the company was hardly cheerful except for a couple of elderly ladies in one corner who looked as though they were conducting a committee meeting and seemed very much at home. Maybe the pleasant waiting room was more inviting than their own places. Trouble had been taken to make it comfortable, though he hoped the medical team took better care of their patients than their plants. Green leaves were making a desperate effort at the end of long spindly stalks growing out of dusty earth.

Hunter entertained himself for a few minutes reading the notice-board where colourful posters warned him of the dangers of glue-sniffing, unprotected sex and the consumption of animal fats. A hand-written card advertised a self-help group for back sufferers. Hunter passed some time inventing self-help groups for policemen, sufferers from sleep deprivation, perhaps, or from

133

marital problems caused by having to go on duty when you'd promised to take the children out. He noticed that the *Readers' Digest* was still top favourite as time-passing reading matter.

There was an undefinable smell, not exactly antiseptic. Perhaps, Hunter decided, it was the smell of disease and discomfort and depression. He looked around him and wondered why a small table stood against the far wall, at a distance from both the receptionists' counter and the patients' chairs, holding nothing. Above it, a smaller notice-board gave phone numbers for information on various diseases, mostly the sort you would hesitate to discuss with a doctor who was also a personal acquaintance. Next, he speculated on the great bite taken out of the lower part of the backrest of each chair. Its purpose was certainly not decorative. Maybe it was to do with the physical laws of stress that allowed the plastic to accommodate itself to the various shapes and sizes of posterior placed on it. Hunter imagined that the way the sections of all but the leanest bulged through to amuse the row behind was incidental rather than planned.

The elderly ladies, having asked solicitously after each other's symptoms and exchanged progress reports, were now proprietorially offering each other snippets of apocryphal information about Fenwick's private life. One of them claimed to know intimate details of his current love affair. Hunter watched her as she revealed all in a stage whisper. The skin hung below her strong jawbone, making her look like a poorly printed picture where the lines of the drawing are distinct but the printed patches of colour are badly placed and spill over the outline. Her companion was not entertained by the revelations she was being offered and interrupted them with loud complaints about the length of time she had been waiting. She was just out of Hunter's line of vision. He shifted slightly and saw a face so dominated by its mouth that the other features seemed added merely as a decoration to it. Square horse teeth filled it, the chin receded from it, a small button nose and currant eyes, almost browless, ornamented it. In spite of the heat, her body, the pillow on which it rested, was swaddled in layers of clothing. If she needed to take them off for a physical examination she alone would put the appointments another quarter of an hour behind.

'Mr Clark to see Dr Blake,' announced a voice on the intercom. No one rose to obey the summons and the assembled company avoided each other's eyes as they disclaimed collective responsibility for his non-appearance.

Hunter became aware that a child who had come in after him with her mother and a baby was now standing in front of him and he recognised Priestley's helpful young neighbour. 'Tell the gentleman your name,' her mother urged her, with a look that reproached Hunter for his omitted enquiry.

'S'mamfer,' muttered the child and wiped her sleeve across her still runny nose.

'Is this your baby sister?' asked Hunter, dutifully, pinning his faith on the significance of a pink jacket. The baby was offered for his approval and he leaned over to look, expecting pudgy features. He was surprised to find she was like a baby in a medieval picture with minute but adult features and expression. He bit back the awaited, 'She's lovely,' and sought something more worthy of this small individual. 'She's very dignified,' he said, eventually. 'She's herself.' The mother looked affronted and Hunter reflected sadly that the baby would soon become another Samantha.

A further ten minutes passed before he was eventually allowed to see Christopher Fenwick, but he was a sight worth waiting for with his fair crew cut and sunglasses. He wore aquamarine cotton pants and a sort of overblouse with ribbed welts of the same hue and cheerful overchecks. White trainers completed the effect of cool and casual efficiency. He grinned as he read Hunter's opinion in his face. 'I look even more absurdly youthful in formal dress and that destroys the confidence of the old ladies.'

The surgery providing a background for this unexpected doctor was plain and conventional. The plants here flourished and the soulless cube was made friendlier by a busy clutter of correspondence, reference books and files. These had been tucked behind a curtain but had fallen sideways towards the middle of the window-sill. The hand-basin had cupboards above and the surface into which it was set held a yellow plastic box, a bag of cotton wool balls, various jars with learned labels and a round container of tongue depressors that turned Hunter's knees to jelly. He stifled a sudden memory of a consultation when he was six years old with a GP whom he'd been convinced was attempting to choke him to death as he'd innocently tried to avoid the young Hunter's teeth and get a glimpse of his enlarged tonsils.

Further along were a calculator and a jar of syringes in sterile

135

solution. Hunter let his gaze rest on these with equanimity. He'd prefer a hundred injections to one attempt to examine his throat. The walls here were cool and plain, the only fixture being a huge roll of absorbent paper over the couch, so that no patient examined on it actually had to make contact with the hideously patterned blanket that covered it. An Anglepoise lamp was fixed to cast maximum light on areas patients would, doubtless, prefer to keep hidden.

Fenwick invited Hunter to sit in his patients' chair and regarded him critically. 'With my doctor's hat on I advise you to remove your jacket and tie before you die of heatstroke.' Hunter smiled and did so. 'I shall now remove that headgear and don what is suitable for a witness.'

'You'd better wear one on top of the other,' Hunter told him. 'You're a witness because you're the medic in the case.'

Fenwick nodded. 'Before you begin your questions, can I just ask if there's any news of Anne-Marie? Theresa's almost out of her mind with worry. I kept her working until lunchtime thinking that was the best thing for her but I had to send her home this afternoon. She was quite distraught. I rang to ask Christine Morgan to keep an eye on her but I haven't heard from either of them since.'

Hunter shook his head. 'I'm afraid not. We don't really think it's any more than a variation on her usual self-dramatisation but in the circumstances we're treating her disappearance very seriously and have mounted a full-scale search. We could well do without it. There's plenty else for our men to do. What do you as a doctor think of Anne-Marie?'

'She's my patient, you know.'

'Well, of course she is or the question wouldn't apply. Don't give me all that Hippocratic oath nonsense. Presumably you agree that the sooner this business is cleared up, whatever the outcome, the sooner the whole family can get back to something like a normal life – if they've ever had one, that is.'

Fenwick shrugged. 'All right, I'll tell you everything I know that might be relevant.' He plunged into a history of Theresa's childhood, marriage and child-rearing problems that was becoming familiar to Hunter. He had not revealed his personal acquaintance with the family on his last visit to the surgery and chose not to do so now, but let the recital, which had reached Anne-Marie,

136

continue. 'She comes into the centre quite regularly and picks up all the leaflets we have on drugs, sexual abuse, sexually transmitted diseases and so on. She writes that diary of hers in public and leaves it around because she wants it to be read. You'd sit up and blink if you saw it.'

'I've got it in my pocket. I told you we were taking her disappearance seriously.'

Fenwick looked startled. 'Neither Theresa nor I can decide whether it's harmless and she'll grow out of the need for it, or whether she ought to be referred to a psychiatrist.'

'Tell me about her mother.'

Fenwick's expression became obstinate. 'What about her?'

'What are her duties here and how does she perform them?'

His face cleared. 'Oh, that's simple – or complicated – according to how you look at it. She's the practice manager. That means she's in charge of everything that goes on here apart from the diagnosis and treatment of the patients' diseases. Notice I didn't say "patients' problems". A lot of them come here for family and social reasons and Theresa deals with a lot of those. In addition she oversees the work of the cleaning staff and receptionists, keeps an eye on the paperwork, is responsible for all the finance. You think of it, Theresa does it, from switching off the burglar alarm when she opens up to switching it on again when she leaves.'

'It sounds pretty demanding.'

'It doesn't demand too much of Theresa, at least not under normal circumstances.'

'So, she's resourceful and efficient?'

'Extremely.'

'Yet she had to humour and keep her husband and can't escape from being dominated by her mother?'

Fenwick sighed deeply. 'Everyone's dominated by her mother, including the vicar and myself. My heart sinks when she walks into the surgery. She makes her progress from the door to that chair that you're sitting in with a suggestion of a limp, just a hint which, together with her pained expression, indicates not an infirmity of the legs and feet but what she sees as her pitiable need for sympathy and understanding. She thinks she's dying of criminal neglect and bowel cancer. Actually she's suffering from paranoia and piles!' Hunter laughed. 'On the other hand, the heart problem, which is genuine, she makes very little fuss about.'

137

'I see.' Hunter felt for his tie and looked surprised to find it wasn't there. 'Was it a recurrence of her heart trouble that landed her in hospital on July the thirty-first?'

'I think so, though it may have been a bug of some kind that aggravated it. When I saw her she was having cold sweats and abdominal pain. She was dizzy and confused and uncoordinated. Her heartbeat was irregular and she was short of breath. I suspected some kind of virus or infection because areas of her skin were reddened, especially on her hands and face, but apparently no rash developed and once in hospital she recovered quite quickly though they kept her in for a few days to run some checks. They didn't find anything except the angina we already knew about.'

'Would you mind writing all that down for me – the notes on Mrs Kelly's card perhaps, but in a form that we can understand?'

'I'm not sure.' He frowned. 'What do you want it for?'

'I don't have to tell you that but it might help us both if I do. We very much want to know why Mrs Kelly rang her daughter for help at a few minutes after nine but you weren't sent for until about an hour later, by which time she claims she was recovering.'

Fenwick's eyes widened. 'What are you talking about? Theresa rang me at about ten o'clock, said she thought her mother had had a slight heart attack and could I please come at once. I did. Theresa said the symptoms had developed rapidly and she'd rung at once because she knew her mother needed to be in hospital.'

The two men contemplated each other for some seconds before Hunter resumed his questions. 'Was Mrs Carr more on edge or frightened than was to be expected considering her mother's indisposition?'

Fenwick considered. 'Come to think of it, yes, she did seem more shaken than I would have anticipated. After all, she's quite used to medical crises and this was not her mother's first attack. I wondered at the time if she felt guilty because it was brought on by some family disagreement. The boy was there and he doesn't submit to his grandmother's authority like Theresa and Anne-Marie do.'

'What exactly is your relationship with Mrs Carr?'

Fenwick looked first astonished and then angry. 'What the hell are you getting at? Theresa was, until a couple of weeks ago, a respectable married woman who took her marriage vows extremely seriously. She's years older than me – old enough to have more sense than to accept overtures from a punk doctor.'

'You made some, then?'

'No, I bloody well didn't! Whatever gave you that idea? She's the ideal practice manager and I wouldn't dream of jeopardising an excellent business arrangement nor my engagement to an ideal future wife for a doctor.'

'Mrs Kelly gave me the idea,' Hunter told him in a rather more placatory tone. 'She told me you accompanied Mrs Carr to the hospital on Sunday afternoon, partly because you realised what was due to her as your patient and partly because you were attracted to her daughter.'

Fenwick gave a mirthless laugh. 'The Kelly woman again! I took Theresa to the hospital because she was determined to go. She is a valued colleague and friend and she wasn't at all well. She'd fainted over breakfast and been unable to attend morning church. The boy was playing in his match and I couldn't dissuade her from going so I accompanied her.'

He began to clear his desk in a dismissive fashion with quick angry movements. Hunter touched his arm to catch his attention. 'Sergeant Hunter has to ask such questions. Mr Jeremy Hunter has better manners and dislikes asking them as much as you dislike being asked.'

Fenwick grinned. 'OK. I have to ask some pretty obnoxious questions myself.'

'I've two more, I'm afraid. Both arise out of extracts from Anne-Marie's diary. Have you any reason to suspect that Mrs Carr was ever struck or otherwise physically abused by her husband?'

'None whatsoever. In my opinion it wasn't in his character and I've worked at pretty close quarters with Theresa. I've seen absolutely no evidence of it. What's the other question?'

'Was there any sexual abuse of Anne-Marie by her father?'

There was a considerable pause but then Fenwick shook his head. 'No. I stopped to consider because I'd never thought about the possibility. After a brief but serious consideration of it I think it's extremely unlikely. There's one other thing though. Frank came in yesterday and asked me to describe in detail the effects of swallowing nicotine.'

'Yesterday?'

'That's right. I'd hardly have waited so long to tell you if he'd asked me before his father died.'

Hunter nodded, made a further note, then rose to go. At the door he paused. 'You're not a punk, are you?'

Fenwick's grin broadened. 'Not technically, but you try explaining that to the old biddies you've been sitting with out there.'

Chapter 15

Mitchell, fast running out of enthusiasm for the task in hand, knocked on his twenty-third door of the afternoon. He had not dared to garb himself in vest and shorts as Hunter had half imagined he might, but the old man who answered his knock was not impressed by his open-necked, short-sleeved shirt and light cotton trousers. He peered closely at the identification Mitchell offered him. 'You don't look much like a bloody policeman to me. They were smart young chaps in my day. Any road, you'd best come through. Medway's the name.'

He had gone ahead through the narrow hall and opened the garden door. 'Come out the back. You can ask your bloody questions as well in a deck chair as an easy chair in't bloody parlour.'

Mitchell followed him outside and looked round him admiringly. The arrangement of plants in blocks and rows was rather regimented for his taste but the profusion of colour and perfume was impressive. 'I can see why you want to spend your time out here, sir.'

'It's none so bad.' The old man acknowledged the compliment with a satisfied smile. 'I've a kind young friend who does the heavy digging now.'

Mitchell took the deck chair Medway had fetched from the shed, set it up and sank into it, glorying in his luck. This was the man he had been longing to question ever since another late session at the library had established that the chief users of nicotine were the tobacco industry and the manufacturers of gardening products. He could have looked him out deliberately, but apparently working on your own initiative was now a sin in old Browne's book. Mitchell couldn't decide whether age was making the inspector crabby or whether he was coming under the influence of stuck-up Hunter. Anyway, now Providence had given him his witness whilst he was in the course of obeying Browne's instructions implicitly. 'Would that be Frank Carr, by any chance?'

The old man's eyes twinkled. 'Sharper than you look, aren't you?' Did he not look sharp? Mitchell bridled. 'What is it you want with me then?'

For the twenty-third time, Mitchell went into his explanation. 'We're asking everyone in the street if they noticed Gary Carr come out of the Rag and Louse at about five past eight on the night he disappeared and if they know which way he went.'

The old man looked triumphant. 'You've struck lucky then. He come out as I was going in. He spoke to me in fact and then the rest of us went in to talk about that bloody cricket match that nivver got finished. I had a good chinwag to Walt Crossley and Ben Poskitt. We were hoping for great things from Ben. He's ungainly built but a neat mover. Reminds me of Tom Graveney a bit.'

Mitchell's excitement was mounting. 'Can we go back a bit? What did Gary Carr say to you?'

Medway grinned reminiscently. 'He weren't best pleased. I asked him where he were rushing off to so early and he answered, sarcastic like, "up to London to look at the queen". I cottoned on like and asked him if he were going to frighten a little mouse. He said, no, he were going to accept some more sodding charity. I expect he meant that bloody Kelly woman. Why old Francis had to marry her, I shall nivver know.'

'Why charity? Was she in the habit of subsidising the Carr family?'

'Aye, there'd be a hand-out now and again when she wanted them to feel grateful. It gets young Frank's goat and Carr wasn't a scrounger except for letting his wife keep the household going, not the sort to hang around in the pub waiting to be treated. She often gave them stuff they didn't want anyway. Carr took it so as not to make trouble for young Theresa by refusing and offending her.' He chuckled. 'Mebbe he was going to get the gardening things she got young Frank to fetch from my garage, keeping 'er heirlooms in t'bloody family.'

'Maybe he was. What exactly did Frank take away, Mr Medway?'

He paused to recollect. 'A wheelbarrow, a watering can, some shears and a damned good spade and fork that'll last till kingdom come. Not that I ever used 'em, mind, but I oiled 'em from time to time in Francis's memory. He wouldn't lie easy in his grave if his tools got rusty. There were a box of bits an' bats too.'

'What sort of bits and bats?'

He wrinkled his brow. 'I can't rightly remember all on 'em. Stuff we used for capsid bugs.' He named the creatures with venom in his voice. 'Bloody pests!'

'What harm do they do?' Mitchell hoped the floodgates he was opening would pour forth vital information along with the old man's obsessions.

'What harm? They're death to all fruit bushes, specially black-currants. Hatch out in April and make brown spots and holes in the young leaves. Then they attack the terminal buds and masses of bloody side shoots develop. They cause brown and yellow patches on the gooseberries and make the bloody skins crack. When they're young you can see through the bloody things and they feed on weeds but they're bright green when they're fully grown . . .'

Mitchell stretched in his deck chair. The sun beat down on his head and he tried to keep his eyelids from drooping as the voice droned on. '. . . winter washing with a good tar distillate, then spray with DNC petroleum wash at seven and a half per cent early in March. Then you spray with nicotine late in April and again in mid May.' Mitchell sat up. 'They're canny little buggers. When they feel a jar on the tree caused by the spray they drop to the ground to feed on the weeds again so you have to spray the ground as well as the trees. Then you put a band of grease round the tree trunks to stop the beggars climbing up again. They do chrysanths a power o'no good an' all. Of course there's all kinds of fancy new methods of killing 'em off now but the old 'uns'll do for me.'

'What kind of nicotine compound do you spray with?'

'Well, Francis had a bloody great greenhouse and for that we used liquid nicotine, one-sixth of a fluid ounce to the same amount of meths to a thousand cubic feet. We vapourised it in a pan over a spirit lamp.' He was carried away, oblivious of the effect he was having on Mitchell. 'Sucking insects that don't eat leaves and stems can only be controlled by contact sprays so we used soft soap for that. One pound dissolved in a drop of warm water. Then we lobbed in one ounce of ninety-eight per cent nicotine and made the solution up to ten gallons.'

Mitchell was staggered. 'But didn't you have trouble obtaining nicotine in job lots?'

'Nay, it weren't nicotine that were hard to get hold on. It were bloody soft soap. Sometimes we had to use . . .'

'Never mind that. Tell me about the nicotine.'

'No problem. It had to be bought from a chemist's where you were known. Francis signed the Poison Book. Mind, I'm going back a bit. He's been dead a fair few years.'

'So how much nicotine do you think was kicking about in your box of bits and bats?'

Mr Medway looked annoyed. 'Kicking about? You aren't accusing me of being bloody irresponsible, I hope. I warned young Frank when he took the stuff that there was a jar of powdered nicotine and an inch of liquid left in t'bottle. They were both clearly labelled and the lids firmly on. What more was I supposed to do?'

'How about locking it up and refusing to let Frank have it?'

He spluttered. 'But that's just what I bloody well wanted to do. My garden's just like a pocket handkerchief compared with the one Francis had. There was enough stuff left in that box to serve my bloody purpose indefinitely.'

Mitchell rose and excused himself. 'And to serve Master Frank's purposes,' he muttered to himself as he closed the front garden gate behind him. Then he remembered that, according to Bellamy, Charles Atkinson too, in his temporary employment, had easy access to gardening products.

Sitting in the interview room in his formal shirt and tie, his shoes carefully polished and his expression sullen, Frank seemed, to Jennie Smith, to be a different boy from the grubby cheerful lad who had returned from Mr Medway's garden to talk to her and Mitchell. The inspector was making little progress with him. He had decided to defend himself by saying nothing in spite of the encouraging nature of Browne's opening remarks. The inspector suspected that it was because the boy didn't know what to say, rather than a positive wish to be uncooperative. The sullenness

144

seemed born of fear and misery rather than resentment and aggression. If this boy had committed any punishable offence then he had been driven to it and for reasons which seemed good to him. For those who had driven him, Browne determined that there should be a just retribution. His face was pinched and drawn and the fresh colour had gone from it, so that the odd blemishes on the youthful skin were prominent.

But he looked angry as well as frightened and Browne dared not discount the chance that this youth had struck in defence of those he considered less able than himself to cope with the problems Gary Carr had caused them. He smiled grimly. Both the mother and the sister had found their own way of escape. This boy was more vulnerable than they were because he shared the sufferings of all feeling creation. Browne contemplated him, remembering the scraps of information about him offered by his family and friends, the fascination with ants, the reluctance to beat another boy in a race, the willingness to help an old man whose enthusiasms had outlasted his bodily strength.

He sighed. The boy wasn't going to talk and he couldn't face coaxing him through yet another recital of the festival proceedings. He decided direct questioning was being cruel to be kind. 'I gather you're a quick thinker,' he remarked, regarding the bowed head and lowered eyes, 'but you'll be wasting your time if you invent any dead rats or bitches on heat to put me off the scent.' The boy coloured but refused to look up or reply. 'How do you explain a piece of polythene, torn from a wheelchair bag, being found in the spinney the other Sunday morning?'

The shoulders shrugged almost imperceptibly. 'I nicked one,' he muttered, 'from the garage when the church grounds were being cleared for the festival.'

'It strikes me as a bit big and unwieldy for a litter job.'

'Yes, it was.' The reply was addressed to the surface of the table between them. 'It didn't turn out to be much use. We ended up using smaller ones.'

'Why do you think we've impounded your car?' Browne demanded suddenly.

Again the shoulders moved slightly. 'I expect you have your reasons.'

The telephone rang, making all three of them jump. Browne

listened, replaced the receiver and stood up. 'I have to leave you for a few minutes.'

He went out and Frank looked up tentatively to find Jennie smiling at him. Neither of them spoke.

When Browne returned, he carried a tray from which he dispensed three cups of tea. 'I've been receiving reports from Sergeant Hunter and Constable Mitchell. Perhaps you'd like to tell us what made you ask Dr Fenwick about the effects of swallowing nicotine.'

After a silence of about thirty seconds, Browne repeated his question. Frank forced his glance to meet Browne's. 'I wanted to know whether my father had suffered very much.'

Horrified by what he read in the boy's eyes, Browne steeled himself to continue. 'We found a scrap of paper in the spinney with a list of names in your handwriting.'

The voice was flat and expressionless. 'I dare say you did. I made about a dozen lists for the cricket team. I'm sorry for making litter.'

'Why a dozen?'

'We wanted to win. I kept rearranging the names and people kept changing their minds about whether they could play. Some people said we couldn't use boys who only came to youth club and not to church. I didn't know whether to count them in or not.'

Browne nodded. 'Constable Mitchell's been talking to Mr Medway. What did you do with the box with the pest killer in it that you took from his garage for your grandmother?'

Frank sipped his tea, swallowing with difficulty. 'I didn't know exactly what the box had in it. I left it with all the other stuff in the garage where I work in Archer Road.'

'Not at your grandmother's flat?'

'Where could she keep it?'

'You tell me.'

'Sergeant Hunter's been there. Ask him if she's got the space.'

'Then why not your own house?'

'We haven't room either. Our garage only just takes the Mini with the three bikes and we couldn't keep a wheelbarrow in the house. Mr Mellor said they'd be all right at the garage till Gran had decided who was having them.'

146

'Very convenient for you.'

The boy's face whitened. 'I don't know what you mean.'

'No? Maybe you will when we see whose prints are on the jar and bottle. We'll make you as comfortable as we can in the meantime.'

Chapter 16

Browne paused long enough to despatch Bellamy to Mellor's garage, then set off in his own car through back streets and on to the narrow road up the valley side above Crossley Bridge. He could see the clear paths of the canal and the river which for a while flowed parallel. Even up here the light glinted on the water where his view of it was not obstructed by tall buildings, mills and tower blocks clustered in the valley bottom. The road he had travelled snaked down to them. He watched a car, labouring up it, meet another cautiously descending. The tortuous bends were necessary to allow traffic a reasonably safe descent. At least in August the cobbles gave a firm grip. In December snow and ice were additional hazards, so many feet above sea level. Maybe global warming would have some compensations in Cloughton. He thanked a Providence whose existence he sometimes doubted for protecting the trees that relieved the dismal mixture of brick, stone and concrete below and throwing up a chequered backcloth of rough grass and scrub.

The pleasure he usually found in these surroundings was absent today as he mulled over his interview with Frank. Presently he turned off the road into a cobbled yard and parked in front of a terrace of three cottages, the middle one sporting a well-polished brass knocker on a door of a cheerful crimson.

When Gerald Morgan let him in, Browne looked around him with interest. His dating of the building was no more precise than 'very old'. Dark beams punctuated a white plaster ceiling. The problem of sloping ground had been resolved by means of four deep steps in the middle of the huge room which constituted the ground floor. On the lower level a back door opened into a kitchen area, sectioned off by waist-high wooden screens. The steps led through an arch, which revealed the thickness of what

148

had originally been a dividing wall, to an area containing easy chairs. Browne could see out to a garden that continued upwards to a skyline above the level of the window. The furnishings were austere. The bare plaster walls were painted white, the floor was of polished wood. A piano on the lower level was bare-topped. There were no plants and few pictures, the only splash of colour coming from the dust jackets in a well-filled bookcase.

The house was a fitting setting for its owner. Gerald Morgan's features were like his brother's but he wore them with a more ascetic air. His hair was neatly clipped though just as curly as Glyn's, but the brows were sleeker and the expression more serious though just as eager. He looked like a monk till he smiled and dimples appeared. Browne couldn't remember ever before having seen them in such a fleshless face and he thought it was a pity this man had had the task of producing his play. He would have looked superb as the saint himself.

Not knowing precisely what he wanted Morgan to tell him, Browne followed his usual procedure and just let him talk, telling him, to get him started, that he had heard only praise for the writing, casting and performance of the pageant.

Morgan pulled a wry face. 'It seemed a good idea when it first struck me. I'd done productions at school – yes, I'm another teacher – and I was of the fond opinion that adults would be easier to manage than children, less excitable and pushy and more able to follow instructions and remember lines. Such touching faith! All the people who wanted to be in it were quite unsuitable and the really good people were full of excuses why they couldn't manage it. I looked on lesson reading in church as auditions. Anyone who can make a cracking job of an account of an Old Testament battle has usually got what it takes. Then, just when the last part was given out, second thoughts started occurring and people dropped out and before long we were back to square one. It's funny how scarce religious plays are – good ones, that is – and we didn't fancy all that effort if the script wasn't worth while. You should have seen some of those that people offered to lend me.'

Not a modest man, Browne noted.

'The story of our patron saint lent itself to drama. He was archbishop of both York and Worcester and the legend has it that he died in that office, just after fulfilling the daily Lenten observance of washing the feet of twelve poor men and serving them at table. That made a good scene. He was the first English royal saint but he was excluded from the throne during the reign of Edwin of Northumbria and took refuge among the Scots who converted him to Christianity. That was easy to dramatise too. He was distinguished as a Christian soldier and defeated Caedwalla.' Browne feared that asking about Caedwalla would put paid to the rest of his evening. 'Before the battle, Oswald erected a cross and supported it with his own hands whilst it was being made fast in the earth. That—'

'—made a good scene,' Browne finished for him.

Morgan grinned. 'It did. That was the first symbol of faith to be erected in Bernicia.'

'Really?'

Morgan looked to see if he were being mocked. Browne continued, hastily, 'I gather the Carr children were two of your actors.'

His face cleared. 'That's right. Anne-Marie's a superb actress. Oswald's page sounds unimportant but it's actually a major rôle in my piece.'

'And Frank?'

'Frank can't act but he learns his lines conscientiously and speaks them intelligently.'

'Someone, Zoe, I think, told me he was St Aidan.'

'That's right. When St Oswald had established his kingdom he sent to Iona for a bishop to teach his subjects. Aidan came and Oswald was his interpreter as he preached. One Easter Day, Oswald sat at dinner with the bishop by his side.' Browne sighed and tried to concentrate. 'A servant announced the arrival of a great number of beggars. Oswald sent out the great silver dish in front of him. The contents were distributed and then the dish itself was divided between them. Aidan took Oswald's right hand and said, "May this hand never perish".'

'That must have made . . .'

Morgan took the teasing in good part. 'Yes, it made an excellent scene. It also had the makings of a first class row.'

Browne no longer found it difficult to concentrate. 'Tell me about that.'

'Well, eight years later, Oswald was killed at the Battle of Maserfield and his head and limbs were nailed to a tree. "Oswald's tree" gives us Oswestry.'

Browne nodded acknowledgement of this gratuitous information. 'A year later, the head was buried at Lindisfarne and the arms and body at Bamburgh. It was said that the hand that Aidan had blessed was still uncorrupted.'

'And the row?' Browne prompted him, impatiently.

'Well, Zoe wanted to know where he'd be at the Resurrection if his remains were scattered in so many different places and that started Priestley off complaining to Philip about filling innocent young heads with Popish superstitions. There was quite a barney, which, I suspect, was just what Zoe had intended.'

'So, Mr Priestley wasn't one of your actors?'

'No, the job wasn't that difficult, thank goodness. He thoroughly disapproved and opted out like he does out of most of our social activities. You should hear him go on if someone organises a raffle. Still, if it makes him feel good to make these self-righteous negative gestures, then I defend to the death his right to do so. He calls it "keeping himself from the world"; I call it Puritanic egoism. What's the difference? I don't support the things he organises either. I object to services where six lines of a seven line chorus are "I belong to Jesus", and the seventh is "I belong to Jesus now". Then he makes his ominous ascent to the pulpit with no notes. He reads a text and rambles on about it and regards the free association of ideas as inspiration because he can't feel the mechanics of it.'

Browne thought it was time to divert the flow. 'You didn't consider my colleague as one of your Thespians?'

'Jerry? Not really. He'd be quite good but the sort of work he does makes him too unreliable. It's a shame because he's got plenty of interesting ideas.' He chuckled. 'He does have an outlet for them, though. Annette is the chairperson of the social subcommittee of the PCC and most of the schemes she presents to it are his. It doesn't matter because she presents them very forcefully as her own. In fact, as soon as she realises what good ones they are, she becomes convinced that they are her own. It's a convenient arrangement. It would be a pity if Annette's talent for getting any group of people to agree to all her plans were frustrated by a lack of plans to suggest.'

Browne winced, then embarked on an attack of his own. 'What exactly is your relationship with Theresa Carr?'

He dropped his bantering manner and spoke seriously. 'I'd

marry her tomorrow if she'd have me – though if she mourns Gary long enough for that neurotic child to grow up and leave home, I suppose I could be consoled. Is there any news of her?'

Browne shook his head.

'She'll turn up when her reappearance will have maximum dramatic effect.'

Browne was becoming angry. 'Perhaps you're judging her by your own standards.'

'I'm not judging her at all, though I freely admit that I don't like her. I wouldn't be at all surprised to hear, in a few years' time, that she's given the definitive performance as Lady Macbeth or Desdemona. The trouble is, she behaves like a leading lady now. I wish Theresa would realise she's like this because of her temperament and not because she's had an unhappy childhood. I don't think she has, anyway. Oh, by the way, Priestley's been agonising to me because he thinks he's suspected of doing away with Gary to make life easier for Theresa.'

'Are you telling me Priestley discusses his worries with you?'

'Oh, yes. He likes to be persecuted by the world. I told him that, considering the way he preached at Gary whenever he saw him, it would be more likely for Gary to have done away with him.'

Browne had arranged for the team on his case to pool their ideas in his office at a quarter past six. He glanced at his watch but a small dazzling disturbance in his vision prevented him from focusing on it. He managed to register that it was six o'clock on the larger face of the wall clock behind him, but an aura of brightness surrounded it and the right hand edge of it was blacked out. He recognised with a sinking heart the onset of one of his occasional bouts of migraine and reviewed his plans for the evening. He particularly wanted to give all aspects of the case a thorough airing at this point. He could feel the excitement that arose when he knew a case was nearing its climax. In his mind, he still could not fish out from all the many theories about the case that were floating there the one that fitted all the facts that they'd turned up, but his instinct – or subconscious or whatever, whose promptings he was familiar with – told him that he was approaching the resolution of his difficulties. He considered continuing his schedule as planned but admitted to himself that the effort would be pointless. Once an attack started there was little he could do to prevent it developing and he knew that in another hour he would be feeling too ill to conceal it. He always tried to make as little of these attacks as possible. A recurring and debilitating complaint would do his promotion prospects no good.

He went over to open the window and let in more air. The bright sun danced on the chrome fittings of the vehicles parked outside and dazzled him, making him feel dizzy and sick. He half drew the curtain and sat at his desk, his temples resting in the hollows of his palms. The imminence of a solution to the case gave him little satisfaction. Whoever turned out to be guilty, they had interviewed a great many people whose problems and unhappiness made it possible that they might have killed. Finding the killer wouldn't help them and the killer himself would be uprooted, incarcerated and later regrafted on to society. What use would it all have been?

Hunter came in and Browne tried to share his thoughts, explaining his hollow feeling of futility. What a desolate word that was. Hunter sat down looking startled at the tenor of his chief inspector's remarks. 'Dozens of men have spent a fortnight following up one death. In that time the traffic police have probably dealt with half a dozen, cancer will have accounted for more, drug dealers will have snuffed the spirit out of a streetful of youngsters and, maybe, by tomorrow the IRA will have bumped off half the population of the town.'

Hunter's brow puckered. 'Well, Gary Carr wasn't exactly a public benefactor but he wasn't all bad. Anyway, we can't let the killer off and sanction the deliberate annihilation of a fellow human being.'

Browne was too distressed to try to follow Hunter's logic. He sighed. 'I don't know why we're taking all this trouble.'

Hunter looked alarmed. 'You need either a cup of tea and a few hours' sleep or a drastic replanning of your career.' He looked harder at the inspector's white face and tightened mouth. 'Are you all right, sir?'

Browne's vision was clearing now and his headache was as yet only a dull throbbing in his temple. He managed a wan grin. 'Nothing to worry about. I'm just starting a migraine but I'll be worse before I'm better. I think we'll postpone this session till first thing tomorrow. By then we may have some prints from the pesticide bottles and Anne-Marie may have turned up. I'll get home for a couple of hours in bed and mull over these reports

153

later on. You can type up your notes on what Fenwick had to say and then get off yourself.'

'I'll drive you home first, sir.' Greatly daring, Hunter slipped the file of papers from under Browne's arm and placed them back on his desk. 'I'd leave these here for tonight.'

During the journey home, Browne's headache ripened and as Hunter turned into his drive his stomach began to churn alarmingly and nausea engulfed him. The car stopped and without waiting to thank Hunter or to greet his wife who had come out to the porch he hurried upstairs to the bathroom.

Taking in the situation at a glance, Hannah raised a hand in salute to Hunter, then went upstairs to darken the bedroom and draw back the sheets. After some minutes, Browne returned to collapse gratefully on to them and accept Hannah's proffered glass of water and the small white pills which he knew, if he'd had any sense, he would have carried with him. He was asleep when Mitchell, unexpectedly released from duty by his superior's indisposition, came to pick up his daughter.

Chapter 17

Anne-Marie peered at her luminous watch face. Eleven minutes past nine. Surely no one would come in here now until morning. She stood up gingerly and stepped out from behind the big square machine, gasping softly as the circulation reasserted itself in her cramped limbs. She put her fingers to her mouth and let the pain appear on her face, so accustomed to playing to an audience that she no longer needed one in order to perform. After a few unsteady steps her legs bore her weight again and she stretched the whole of her body with relief as she listened to the subdued sounds of running water and a muffled television advertising jingle. She unfolded the blanket she had been squatting on, spread it out on the cold lino tiles and lay down across the centre of it, folding the edges over to cover herself.

The little room was in darkness at floor level but light from the corridor outside came dimly from the windows high in the wall, making squared patterns on the ceiling. The machines outlined all round her looked like big angular robots. One of them gurgled and she jumped, then covered her mouth with her hand and widened her eyes, acting out the small shock she had felt.

She couldn't decide whether she'd enjoyed her day in Bradford or not. She'd managed to hide herself successfully in the crowds of shoppers and had come back, lost amongst the commuters, to secrete herself in this little hidey-hole for the second night. She hadn't been able to find much money to take with her, and food, even in the most grotty-looking eating places, was very expensive. Once everybody was asleep she'd have to go foraging again. She was grubby and sticky as well as hungry and she had almost abandoned her plan to follow up that policewoman Jennie's suggestion of trying on clothes in a big store to find out what suited her. Then the pretty dresses in C&A's windows had tempted her in and she'd come back time and again to the changing rooms, having collected another armful of clothes.

She had talked to the young girl in the next cubicle who'd been interested to hear about her mother's having twins after such a long stretch without a new baby and had sympathised with Anne-Marie because Theresa was so preoccupied with babies at a time when a teenager needed her support and attention. She'd have liked to tell her that she'd murdered her father because he'd abused her and was cruel to her mother but the shop-girl who was keeping watch on them all was listening and she might have told somebody. Anne-Marie didn't want finding yet. It was funny that the truth, or near truth, was sometimes more fantastic than pure invention and no one would believe it. He'd only got what he deserved though she was sorry that he'd had to die in such a horrible way. She wondered who was going to loom large in her life and her diary now that her father was dead. It could very well be Frank after that phone call.

She tried to recall the tone of voice in which he'd spoken those chilling words. He'd obviously been discussing his future with his friend, Michael. 'I still might not apply,' he'd said. 'I know one big obstacle's out of the way but there's still Anne-Marie.' She'd puzzled over this at length. Frank was obviously talking about his university plans. How could she be an obstacle? She'd miss his company but she wanted him to go. It would add to her status to have a student brother. Had he poisoned Daddy and then tried to get rid of her? She remembered the night before the body was discovered. She'd been allowed hot chocolate in bed. Her mother had brought it up to her but he had suggested it and he had made it. She thought now that it had tasted bitter. Had she thought so at the time? She knew she had a vivid imagination and now she couldn't be sure. What she did remember for certain was that she'd been very groggy the next morning. She'd woken very late and had had to hurry to be ready in time for church.

She'd been going to take up the hem of her pink skirt but there hadn't been time and she'd had to wear the navy one. It hadn't really mattered. She didn't look right in either of them and none of the clothes she'd tried on today had made her look like Zoe – well, not like her exactly, but they didn't make her look right as Zoe looked right. She hadn't really much idea what she ought to look like. In fact she wasn't a lot of use at being herself. It was

156

quite frightening sometimes. She made a much better job of being someone else.

She'd been good at being Oswald's page. She'd known exactly what he should look like. She'd been able to make suggestions to Mr Morgan about how he'd speak and dress and behave and she'd known that she was quite right. It was all very puzzling really.

She felt in her pocket and fingered the key to Gran's flat. Had her mother missed it yet? If she had she wouldn't necessarily connect it with her own disappearance. She'd creep out and raid Gran's larder again soon. She'd only taken a couple of slices of bread and a piece of cheese and an apple last night and she didn't think Gran would have missed those but tonight she'd need more. She was ravenous. And whilst she was there she'd look for something to cushion her better against the hard floor.

She wondered if Gran had been told she was missing or whether they'd thought it would worry her too much. She felt very warm and loosened her blanket. Of course, the whole of this place was heated up so that the old people wouldn't be cold. Then she lay, her hunger forgotten for a few minutes in the pleasure of imagining the efforts of her family and the police to find her. They'd be sure to have found her diary by now. It should make some of those policemen blink a bit. She hoped someone would show it to Jerry Hunter. Even Zoe would be regretting the things she'd said to her and realising how much she'd miss her if she never saw her again.

It was quite silent now and the daydreams drifted into a doze but her empty stomach soon reasserted its complaints and woke her. It should be safe now. The main corridor lights had been dimmed to the night level and she could hear nothing. She opened the door a crack and looked right down the passage that led to Gran's block.

'Why, Anne-Marie!' exclaimed the warden's voice from the other direction. 'You're never visiting your gran at this hour! And whatever are you doing in the laundry?'

Browne woke up at half-past nine and opened his eyes warily to find the pain had almost gone from behind them. He sat on the side of the bed feeling rather washed out but definitely on the mend and decided there was still part of the day to be used. Hannah heard his movements and called up to offer coffee. Life was looking up. They drank it in the sitting room where Hannah dealt with his intention to return to the station by announcing that she'd hidden the car keys. She was replenishing their cups when the front door slammed and angry footsteps clumped upstairs.

Browne went into the hall. 'Is that you, Virginia?'

'Yes. I'm going to bed.' She appeared on the landing, sponge bag in one hand, towel in the other.

'Is something wrong?'

She tossed her head. 'I don't suppose you'd think so. You've done a good job indoctrinating Benny.'

'With what, for goodness' sake?'

'Oh, as if you need to ask!' She was gone with a swish of cotton skirt and a slam of the bathroom door. Browne returned to his coffee.

After fifteen minutes, Virginia appeared in the doorway, dressing-gowned, pink and shiny, wet hair in black corkscrews. 'I'm sorry I was rude. Benny and I had a row. I don't want to talk about it. How's the head?'

Appeased, Browne poured her a cup of coffee and made room for her on the sofa.

When Browne walked into the station on Friday morning, Hunter was glad to see him looking much his usual self. He paused three steps up on his way to his office on the first floor and regarded his sergeant affectionately. 'Thanks for the sheepdogging last night. Hope I wasn't too much of a bear.'

Hunter nodded, accepting the tacit information that enough had been said and refraining from unnecessary enquiries as to the inspector's present health.

'Anything new?'

Hunter nodded again and followed Browne upstairs. 'Bellamy went round to the garage last night. There was no one there. He tried the phone book for Mellor's private number but that was no go either.'

At the end of Browne's corridor they saw Mitchell already hovering outside his door. Browne wondered if perhaps his night had been as sleepless as Virginia's and what they might have disagreed about.

He unlocked his door as Hunter asked from behind him, 'How soon can we see Anne-Marie?'

Mitchell scowled. 'Bags it's not my job. Stupid little idiot!'

'You don't pick and choose in this business,' Browne snapped at him. Then he moderated his tone. It wouldn't do to let Mitchell think he was being punished for upsetting Virginia. 'You won't have to as it happens. I've got other fish for you to fry.'

Jennie Smith appeared from the stairs, closely followed by Dean from the lift. 'It's useful that the station has facilities for geriatrics,' Mitchell remarked pertly to Dean as they all accommodated themselves around the huge desk.

Browne sighed. A thwarted Mitchell meant a difficult day. 'We won't wait for Nigel,' he began. 'I expect you've all heard that Anne-Marie Carr has turned up. She had hysterics when the warden of the sheltered housing complex who found her tried to drive her home. She was screaming that she wouldn't be safe under the same roof as her brother. No one's sure what it's all about. In the end the warden took her to her grandmother's flat where she managed to calm her down. She rang the girl's mother and the station from there, and Dr Fenwick. He came and sedated the girl and the mother too, I believe. Anne-Marie spent the night with her grandmother, pending a sort-out this morning. Let's thank the Lord, Jerry, for sane children and that's no blasphemy.'

Hunter had taken his usual back-to-front position on an upright chair. 'What exactly are we hoping to get out of her?'

Mitchell rolled up his eyes. 'Nothing that makes any sense, that's for sure.'

Browne quelled him with a glance. 'My superiors and, from what I've heard, some of you seem to think we've enough circumstantial evidence to arrest Theresa Carr or Frank or both. That seems to me a nonsense. I'll make an arrest when I know exactly who did what and there won't be any "or" about it. There's been just one development that you won't have heard. A large suitcase containing Gary Carr's working clothes, tools and the rest of the gear he was supposed to have taken to Harlow has turned up buried fairly deep in Harry Medway's garden. Good thinking there, Mitchell. No one would have thought anything of seeing Frank delving in the soil there and Medway was very unlikely to turn it up himself. Frank of course is denying all knowledge of it. I let him go home last night and I let him go again when I'd seen him this morning. We're not likely to break him here. Right; that's enough from me. What deep thoughts on what aspect of the subject can you dredge up for me, Richard? Begin anywhere you like.'

Dean leaned back in the well-padded armchair he'd appropriated. 'It seems crazy to me that everyone's trying to link up Theresa Carr with someone different. Hunter says it's because she was wasted on her husband and anyone would have been better. The neighbours are buzzing about Alan Priestley. We know that wasn't on but they do seem to have seen a lot of each other for some reason.'

'The mind boggles.'

'Anne-Marie says there was something going on with Gerald Morgan.'

'He confirms that,' put in Browne, 'at least on his side.'

Dean looked surprised. 'Do we make something of that then? The old woman is pushing Fenwick as a suitor.'

Hunter shook his head at this. 'Fenwick certainly doesn't confirm it. He was very short with me when I asked him.'

Dean shrugged. 'Escorting patients' visitors to hospital, even if they are employees, is rather beyond the call of duty. He didn't know then, remember, that Carr was dead. At least, not as far as we know.'

'No, but he knew that Theresa wasn't well. They called him in to her.' As Dean seemed to have concluded his remarks for the moment, Browne nodded to Hunter to continue. 'I think that Theresa was at the end of her tether, whipped on one side by her mother and on the other by her husband and she's just snapped.'

Dean protested. 'If she was driven to attack either of them she'd surely resent her mother more.'

Hunter disagreed. 'She couldn't change a lifetime's attitude to her mother. If she could have done, her problems wouldn't have developed the way they did. Another way out would have been to divorce Gary but her religion forbade that.'

Mitchell broke in uninvited. 'Whatever kind of religion makes someone feel that they can't divorce a man but they can kill him?'

Since no one volunteered to answer this question, Hunter resumed his theories. 'We're pretty certain the body was on the Carrs' property and on various occasions was in the boot of the car between Tuesday and Saturday. I think we can assume they definitely put it in the wood although Forensic didn't find anything to help us in the Mini. The only question seems to be which of them did it and since they were both involved in disposing of the body, it hardly matters. I can't see why we don't arrest them both and leave a jury to decide how they managed it between them and a judge to settle what sentence to give.'

'What I can't work out . . .' began Dean.

'None of the rest of us could hope to,' finished Mitchell, his grin not altogether friendly.

Before Browne had a chance to step in there was a tap on the door and the bony, clipped auburn head of Ledgard appeared round the door. 'Your suspicious death in Silver Street yesterday was a brain haemorrhage,' he announced. 'Everything above board. Nothing to investigate. You look busy. Still cudgelling your brains over the Carr case?'

They nodded. 'We know what happened basically,' Dean explained kindly, 'but we can't prove anything absolutely. We think there's little doubt that Theresa Carr killed her husband on Tuesday night, pushed the body into the car boot and would have got her son to bury it that night if her mother's sudden illness hadn't complicated things.'

Hunter, about to put Dean in his place, was prevented by a half shake of Browne's head.

'Then,' Dean went on confidently, 'when the burst of anger and the energy and courage that went with it had died down, she was paralysed with panic and left it where it was until Saturday night when her neighbour commented on the smell. She had to get rid of it then so she and her son drove it to the spinney and tried to burn it.'

'Bravo,' murmured Browne, 'and yet you were saying there was something you couldn't work out.'

Ignoring the teasing, Dean nodded. 'Yes, why didn't they do a thorough job on the burning and why didn't they bury the remains?'

'I can offer a suggestion.' Ledgard came back from the door. 'If you set fire to a dead body it doesn't burn like sticks on a fire. The dead capillaries will swell with the heat and blood and tissue fluid may boil and cause splitting and blistering of the skin which would be pretty unpleasant to see.

'Then the muscles might tend to contract as they were heated

161

past protein coagulation level and contractions of the arms and legs would result, causing them to jerk inwards.

'If the burning was being done by the man's wife and his teenage son, they probably retreated in horror and fright and couldn't bring themselves to return.'

They absorbed this suggestion.

'What Alan Priestley told us suggests that someone returned on Sunday morning to cover the body at least with leaves,' Browne reminded them. 'Who might have done that? Priestley said he met Frank coming up the track and hustled him back into the service. Does that rule him out?'

'No.' Dean was unwilling to relinquish his suggestion. 'He could have done it earlier and just been loitering on the track keeping watch. Or he might have gone back when the service was finished, although there were more people about then and it would have been risky.'

'It didn't have to be Frank who helped with the disposal of the body,' put in Mitchell. 'It could have been Gerald Morgan, or even Priestley who told us this tale to cover himself.'

'Theresa Carr could have covered the body with leaves during morning service,' Hunter suggested.

'She was ill,' Mitchell objected.

'She might have pretended to be so that she could do it. She insisted on the children going to church, remember.'

Browne was not convinced. 'It would have to have been a good pretence to have fooled Fenwick.'

'Unless he was in on the act,' Hunter countered, but then subsided.

'It's all fascinating, Tom, but it's not getting my work done.' Ledgard rose to leave. 'Keep me posted about how it works out.'

As he departed, Mitchell caught Browne's eye. 'If we accept that Theresa and Frank moved the body, it doesn't rule out someone else doing the poisoning. I've been reading about a fourteen-year-old, Graham Frederick Young, who experimented with poisoning people and he doesn't seem to have been any more off his head than Anne-Marie.'

A sudden movement from Hunter drew everyone's attention. 'It had to be Frank who covered the body with leaves. We found a list of his players for the afternoon.'

'True, but . . .'

'He must have dropped it after nine o'clock on Sunday morning. Tim should have been playing in an open air concert with the school band on the Sunday afternoon. At five to nine we got a call to say it was cancelled because so many members were down with a stomach bug that's going the rounds that there was no way they could play their programme. Frank was one team member short and he cheered when he heard the news and said he'd put Tim in to open with him. If I remember rightly, the list that we found had Tim's and Frank's names at the top.'

There was silence for a few seconds, broken by Browne who was shaking his head at his own unwisdom in following his instincts that went against the evidence. 'I somehow can't see either Theresa or Frank Carr as killers under any circumstances. The one quality that all the murderers I've met or heard about have in common is arrogance. They all thought they could arrange things to suit themselves to the point of concluding someone else's existence. Even those who killed out of fear had an arrogant fear and thought life owed them a safe existence with no insoluble problems. Neither Theresa nor Frank Carr fits. Was there something else, Jerry?'

Hunter nodded. 'Annette happened to remark at breakfast this morning that she'd spent the evening Gary disappeared ringing round the people who'd promised flowers for the festival decorations, checking colours, types, lengths of stem and so on. She rang Theresa at about half-past eight and they chatted for fifteen minutes or so. There was no attempt to cut her short and no mention that she was getting Gary's things packed up.'

'So that helps to confirm our suspicions that Theresa invented the story later and at that point had no idea she'd need one. So if she's our customer it would seem that the murder wasn't premeditated.' He paused to write on the sheet in front of him. 'Right, Benny. It's your turn. If you hadn't sniped at everybody else so much you'd have had it sooner.'

'Sir.' Mitchell accepted the rebuke but looked unabashed. 'Could you turn up that report that Sergeant Hunter asked for, sir? The one from Fenwick about Monica Kelly's condition when he examined her on July the thirty-first.'

Browne obligingly fished out the relevant sheet from his file whilst Mitchell excitedly turned pages in his notebook. Finding the place he wanted, he made small ticks on it as Browne read aloud. ' "She complained of headache and abdominal pain, dizziness and visual disturbance. She was sweating and trembling and more than usually confused. Her heartbeat was irregular and her breathing was short, her blood pressure higher than expected and the pulse slow. She had transient paroxysmal atrial fibrillation. The pupils were constricted . . ." What is it, Benny?'

'Sir, when the path lab report first came, I went and checked on the symptoms of nicotine poisoning and they pretty well tie in with what you've read except that I don't understand "paroxysmal . . ." whatever you said.' He handed over his notebook with his added ticks.

'You mean you think Monica Kelly was poisoned too? That Mrs Carr tried to get rid of both her predators?'

'Well, maybe, sir.'

'Oh, cut the crap, Mitchell.'

There was an astonished silence, followed by Hunter's hysterical, half-strangled giggle at his own interruption. Browne was stricken with remorse. 'Mealy-mouthed', he had called Hunter on one occasion. 'Speak the language of the people,' he had instructed him on another. How dared he use his authority to cause a subordinate to make a fool of himself? He owed him an apology but that would embarrass Hunter more, and he feared irreparable damage had been done to their working relationship.

A remark from Mitchell saved the immediate situation, though whether it was merciful or inadvertent, Browne couldn't decide. 'There was something else, sir. I called on Mr Medway.' He added hastily, 'Not on my own initiative. You told me to ask at the houses on the same street as the Rag and Louse.' Browne bit back his smile and nodded. 'It turns out that he was the chap Carr spoke to as he left the car park.' He repeated the brief and cryptic remarks Carr had made to the old man before he had hurried away.

Browne looked thoughtful and added further notes to his sheet of paper. Then he consulted his watch. 'If no one else has anything useful to say, then I've finished for the moment with everyone but Jerry.'

He made his apology briefly and Hunter forgot his own embarrassment as he tried to alleviate Browne's. His sergeant could only be true to his own nature and played a valuable part in the team's work when he was doing just that. No one else was like him or could see what he could see.

To lighten the atmosphere, he remarked in a less serious tone, 'I gather you've added Superintendent Dalziel to your list of rôle models.'

Hunter grinned at this reference to their common enthusiasm for their fictional counterparts and with relief Browne reached for his phone. 'Park yourself, Jerry, and I'll ring down for some coffee.' The time would not be wasted if it re-established their former mutual friendly respect.

Five minutes later, Browne was in full flow. 'Poirot might be a caricature but in some ways he's a more credible detective then Alleyn or Dalgliesh. He's realistically self-opinionated and aggressive even though his stilted conversation's unlikely. The better writers of detective fiction, stylistically speaking, create unlikely coppers because they use the investigation as a framework on which to hang an expounding of their philosophy, examples of their sensitivity and their observation of the natural and human world. And they let them speak with their own wide vocabulary and articulate expression. Some inspector or superintendent or, preferably, a commander is their hero and they can't resist projecting their own creative artistic nature on to him. Their suspects are subtly drawn, realistic, but their policemen are hard to swallow, too nice, too sensitive. There always has to be a character who expresses, in his conversation or his thoughts, his surprise that this senior policeman is as he is. Their readers don't expect police to be like that because they aren't. Dalziel does something to redress the balance, but Mr Hill's real hero is Pascoe who runs true to the type I'm talking about. Anyway – ' draining his cup – 'this isn't going to get the baby bathed.' Both officers went contentedly back to their work.

Chapter 18

Theresa Carr, thankful to be rid of Fenwick's practice nurse who had volunteered to coax her daughter home, pleaded with her son on behalf of Anne-Marie. 'Try to bear with her when she comes down. She really doesn't know what's going on. However hard it is to bear what's happened and what we've done, we know the facts of the matter and what we have to live with. She doesn't and it must be so much the worse for her.'

The exasperated expression sat uneasily on Frank's good-humoured face but for once he had lost patience with both his mother and his sister. 'She wasn't genuinely frightened about that phone call. She knew I was talking to Michael and she knows that my chief reservation about going away is that it would be five years before I could contribute to the family income and that would make things harder for you and her. That's the only way she's an obstacle and she knows it perfectly well. She's just well launched into a terrified teenager act and I've had enough of it.'

'Don't quarrel with her, Frank. I can't cope with it just now.' She stopped, realising that he too could take no more.

He scowled and kicked moodily at a turned-up corner of the hearth rug. 'There's no point in quarrelling with her. She'd just add being misunderstood and persecuted to the drama. But I'm not sticking around to be the audience. I'll make us some tea and when she comes down I'm off to cut Mr Medway's grass. That's where I'll be when the fuzz come hounding me again.'

'I'll make the tea.' Theresa escaped to the kitchen and by the time the kettle had boiled she had won her battle with the tears on his behalf which would have made him so angry. She carried the tray with its three cups through to the sitting room and, without being asked, Frank went to call his sister from her bedroom. 'If she starts an abject penitence for misjudging her devoted brother, I'll run away myself.'

'You,' his mother told him, with her first genuine smile of the morning, 'will never run away from anything.' She decided that her daughter who, although she might be strange, was not insensitive or unintelligent, would read Frank's mood and behave in a way that he could tolerate.

All three drank their tea in silence, then Anne-Marie began to stack the cups. 'I'll start to prepare lunch when I've rinsed these.' She carried them through to the kitchen. The dutiful daughter rôle was bearable to both Theresa and Frank who abandoned his plan to tend Mr Medway's garden. He began to tackle the crossword on the back of the local newspaper which he had refused to cancel when Theresa had suggested it.

Theresa contemplated Anne-Marie's retreating back. Was her daughter playing a rôle? Or was she behaving naturally when she busied herself with domestic tasks? Was she ever really natural or was Gerald right about her? She remembered the television chat show she had watched with him and his scornful comments on Pearl Merriman's interview with Wogan. 'Her real self, my eye! She was born to act and she never stops, least of all when her audience is seeking the person behind all the rôles.' Would Anne-Marie really turn out to be as talented as Gerald predicted? She found his comments comforting. He didn't like Annie, called her neurotic, but he accepted her for what she was, and seemed to recognise in her a known type. To him she wasn't just a unique, disturbed oddity. She gained no reassurance from those people who told her that her daughter wasn't really different or that she'd grow out of it. On the contrary, she was growing progressively into it.

After a short while, the sounds of splashing water were replaced by the slamming of cupboard doors and the whirring of an electric mixer, then, suddenly, Anne-Marie appeared in the doorway. 'I think,' she remarked slowly, as though she were working it out as she spoke, 'that Gran was the only person who really wanted Daddy to be dead.'

Her mother and Frank were equally aghast.

'What a dreadful thing to say!'

'I hope you didn't talk like that last night when she was good enough to cope with your hysterics.'

They spoke simultaneously and were interrupted by the shrill peal of the telephone. Theresa picked up the receiver and listened, then looked at both her offspring apprehensively. 'It's your grandmother. She sounds upset. She wants me to go over there.'

Anne-Marie groaned. 'She was all right when I left. Can't you tell her no for once? I'm making Yorkshire puddings.' When Theresa and Frank both protested she looked astonished. They had had this conversation before but this time they were speaking each other's lines.

Frank grabbed his denim jacket. 'I'll go and sort her out. You stay and have a proper lunch.'

Theresa hesitated but Anne-Marie smiled and shooed her mother into the hall. 'It's no use, Frank. Mum won't be satisfied till she's seen her. I'll hold lunch till she gets back.' She turned back to her mother. 'We promise not to argue whilst you're away.' They all three smiled as Anne-Marie offered the promise that Theresa had frequently extracted from them throughout their childhood.

When Bellamy reached Archer Road he was dismayed to find Mellor's garage staffed only by Frank Carr. 'Mr Gladwin's out on a breakdown,' the lad informed him, 'and Mr Mellor's on holiday till Wednesday, so they rang me to see if I could fill in this morning, doing a few minor repairs and answering the phone. How can I help you?'

Bellamy eyed the almost new Alfa Romeo parked on the forecourt. 'I wish it could be by selling me that but, since we're both working-class grafters, I'd better get on with the job. Will you show me where the gardening stuff is that Mr Mellor agreed to keep for you?'

Frank's face closed up and he led the way without speaking to the back of the workshop behind him. Bellamy was not astonished to find that there was no wooden box containing jars and bottles of pesticide amongst the various tools piled in the corner. He regarded Frank sternly. 'Is it any use asking you where you've hidden the box?'

Frank looked mulish. 'I haven't touched it. It was here last time I looked.'

Bellamy sighed in exasperation. 'And if we dig up more of Mr Medway's garden?'

'You won't find it there. Or, if you do, it isn't anything to do with me.' Frank looked Bellamy in the eye as he spoke, then dropped his gaze to his boot which was prodding the handle of the upturned wheelbarrow. Bellamy, knowing that Browne had failed to get the lad to admit to anything, saw no point in continuing this confrontation. 'Right, we'll go into the office and you can give me Mr Mellor's address and tell me where I can get in touch with Mr Gladwin.'

Frank shrugged and complied with two of the three suggestions. 'The address Mr Gladwin's gone to is in this log book. There's a telephone number but he's been gone since half-past seven. He could well be on his way back by now.'

Bellamy cursed himself for not checking what time the garage opened and hoped Browne would not find out that Frank had had more than an hour there by himself. As he reached for the phone to ring the number Frank indicated, a brawny man, his shirt open to the waist, appeared in the doorway. He despatched Frank to the forecourt to serve petrol to the motorist who had just drawn up and, in reply to Bellamy's questions, informed him that the wooden box had been missing since before Mr Mellor went on holiday. He had no idea when it had last been there. Mr Mellor had been away for nearly a week and would be back on Wednesday.

'Where's he gone? Have you an address for him?'

'Nothing more definite than Amsterdam.' He pointed to a postcard featuring a well-endowed girl in a Dutch bonnet, pinned to the notice-board above the desk by her right wrist.

'Has the whole family gone?'

'His wife has. They haven't any kids. He might have left his address with a neighbour or somebody.'

Bellamy mopped his face and undid another button of his shirt in preparation for more trudging. He thanked Gladwin who had written out Mellor's home address in a schoolboy hand on a grimy torn envelope, cast a final longing glance at the Alfa Romeo and departed. There was no sign of Frank on the forecourt but, perched on the arm of a wooden bench surrounded by bedding plants in the patch of grass that adjoined the garage, he saw Zoe. She appeared to be weeping but as he approached and she removed her handkerchief from her face, he was relieved to see a caricature of her usual grin, albeit from reddened and swollen eyes.

'Hi!' she greeted him, pulling her halter top a daring bit lower.

He sat virtuously at the other end of the bench where he could hardly see what was revealed.

'What are you doing here then? Is something wrong?'

She shrugged. 'Nothing much. Frank's had to go to boring work and then my parents started a row so I thought I'd come and answer the phone for Frank whilst he was getting on in the workshop. Then I saw Mr G. coming back so I squatted here till he goes again. It's not important. The row, I mean. They quite like a good argument and I sometimes join in, but this time they were whispering and it seemed to have something to do with me. I know when I'm not wanted so I buzzed off.'

'Something to do with you?'

But his quickened interest had put her off. 'Certainly nothing to do with you,' she told him, pertly.

'I'm sorry. I didn't mean to be nosy.' He wondered how many lies a DC told in the course of a day. 'It's just that you seemed upset.'

'Oh, I see.' She grinned. 'It's just my hay fever. I'm making it worse, sitting in the middle of all these flowers, but it's comfortable and a good spying place. I get it from Dad. The hay fever, I mean. Dr Fenwick's going to send us both to an allergy clinic. Dad's worse than me today. I expect that's why he's irritable with Mum. It's only his second really bad attack this year, though. The other was on the Saturday of the pageant. He was quite ill. That's why he missed it and went to bed early. Then, when he'd slept half the evening, he wandered round half the night, playing music and walking about outside. It's stupid going out but you get desperate for some cool air when your nose is all swollen.'

'It sounds as if you had a bad night too.'

'I didn't actually. Whatever was in the air affected him more than me. I only know that he was around because I went to the loo at about three o'clock and I saw him through the landing window, shutting the gate. We had a cup of tea before we both went back to bed. Then I couldn't sleep but that was because I was worrying about that minor third in Dad's anthem. I kept humming the phrase to myself and wishing it was all over.'

Concealing his growing excitement, Bellamy rose casually and raised his hand in salute. 'I've got work to do. I hope Mr Gladwin goes out again and you haven't sneezed in vain.' He left her and, when he looked back, received a thumbs-up sign. Turning further, he saw Gladwin climb into a Mellor's van and start it up.

When it had safely disappeared round the corner, she hurried into the workshop and addressed Frank's feet which were sticking out from under a pick-up. 'I want to talk to you. Has he gone for long?'

'Long enough. What's wrong?' He followed her into the office where she was filling the kettle.

'Nothing exactly but I think my mother's pregnant.'

'She can't be!'

Zoe was indignant. 'Of course she can. She's not ninety even though she dresses like it. She's got quite a lot of life in her at times. Dad doesn't seem too happy about it though. He was wittering on about a new member of the family and the effect it would have on me. He said in the circumstances it was stupid and unnecessary.' Her expression changed suddenly. 'Hey! I hope that doesn't mean he's wanting her to have an abortion. He's not usually so stupid. What's so special about a menopausal baby? They happen and they're usually all right. And does he think I'm so spoilt that I expect them to have no time for anybody except me? They're dead wrong. It'll give them something else to think about whilst I get on with my own life. Anyway, I like babies.'

Bellamy stood in front of Browne's desk, sweating unbecomingly but pleased with himself. 'Yes, sir. I went to the address Gladwin gave me. Place was shut and the neighbours didn't know any more than the garage folk. They thought he had relatives in Bradford but couldn't give any details. The woman next door had had a postcard saying that they were enjoying themselves. It had a photo of the Rijksmuseum but no address. The garage one just said "Wish you were here" with three exclamation marks.'

Browne's face was deadpan. 'Rather negative findings. They don't account for that cat with cream look on your face.'

'Sir, I met Zoe on the bit of council garden next to the garage, skulking and spying till Gladwin had gone and she and Frank could have a bit of slap and tickle.' He grinned as he remembered Zoe's triumphant thumb, then repeated the gist of her remarks. 'So Glyn Morgan was wandering about on the Saturday night, sir.

171

And didn't Zoe say before she went to sleep she heard a car nearby and she'd have thought it was the Carrs except they'd gone to bed? It could have been her father in their own.'

'Wouldn't she have heard him getting it out?'

'She could have been splashing about in the bathroom.'

'Wouldn't he have waited until she'd had plenty of time to settle down?' Bellamy shrugged. 'And what about the smell that was supposed to come from the Carrs' drains?'

By now, Bellamy looked crestfallen. 'Could Christine Morgan have started that story to account for the smell that drifted from their own garage towards next door?' This sounded lame even to himself.

Browne smiled sympathetically. 'Find me a ghost of a motive for Glyn Morgan and I'll look at it again. And, of course, we'll have it all on record.'

Chapter 19

Browne and Hunter spent a baking Friday afternoon poring over
every report on any aspect of the case and found themselves
not a fraction further on. Bellamy reported back on a fruitless
three hours spent talking to such customers of Mellor's garage
as might be, in Gladwin's opinion, sufficiently in his employer's
confidence to have been entrusted with his holiday address. No
one knew it. Browne considered a five day wait unreasonable
in a murder enquiry and had requested the Dutch authorities to
trace the Mellors. With that he had to be content.

He arched his back, stretched his tense neck muscles and, pushing back his chair, walked to the window. He surveyed for some
seconds a view that shimmerd in a haze of heat. Then he turned
back into the room. 'Jerry, we've worked through six days of this
glorious weather and we're having a break. Don't switch your mind
off but, unless something else comes up and I have to recall you,
take your body, your family and your cellphone and go and walk
on those hills.'

Hunter was quite prepared to follow this suggestion as far as
his body and his cellphone were concerned, but he knew that his
wife's idea of a summer day out included a car, a sundress and a
picnic on a tablecloth. Perhaps he'd take Tim. 'What will you be
doing?' he asked out of politeness.

Browne considered. 'I'd like another word with Gladwin,
Morgan senior and Charles Atkinson first thing tomorrow. No, I
don't need you with me. I need you fresh for another week and still
happily married. Then, unless further developments rescue me, I
have to take Hannah shopping. I might do it in Leeds. Ginny was
talking about going and if I don't offer her a lift I might give in
to her request to borrow the car.' They both laughed.

In the event, Browne found himself able to shop in Cloughton,

173

his car safely garaged. Virginia had been chauffeured to Leeds by Mitchell who was, apparently, back in his daughter's favour again. After Virginia's parting offer, he was also in favour with Browne. 'Anything you want from the big bookshops? We'll be doing a round of them. Benny's talked me into starting on my Oxford reading list. If I've got a year to go at it I should get through everything and dazzle them all with my profound knowledge.'

'Unless they issue next year's students with a different one,' Browne countered, then wished he could have bitten his tongue out.

'Just let them try.' Mitchell had been spotted through the window and she had departed, laughing.

By mid-afternoon Mitchell was less than amused. This was his fourth bookshop, his tee-shirt and cotton trousers were sticking to him and he determined that their next stop would be a pub that availed itself of all-day opening, that he was paying, whoever's turn Virginia decreed it was, and that they'd be drinking pints.

They stood in a shelved alcove labelled 'Lit Crit' which was stuffed with books about books that Virginia hadn't read, or at least hadn't studied. What was the point, he asked himself, of reading what some self-styled expert thought about a great work when you hadn't yet made up your own mind about it? He took a volume from the nearest shelf: *Seventeenth-Century Literature – a new survey* by Irving Wakeham. The name rang a bell. Mitchell wondered what this volume had to offer when the rest of the shelf was filled with what had already been published on the subject. Certainly not a swinging off-beat title. There was a photograph of the author on the back cover and, as he studied it, the assistant left Virginia for a moment and fixed her professional smile on him. He offered the picture for her inspection. 'Doesn't look a bundle of laughs does he?'

She grimaced at him. 'I can assure you that he wasn't. He taught me in the sixth form. We used to joke about his name – "I. Wakeham after I've sent 'em to sleep." '

Now Mitchell knew why the name was familiar. The assistant continued her reminiscences. 'He used to make the same jokes day after day. There was a boy in the class with a Welsh sounding name though he was born and brought up in the next street to me. He always addressed him as "bach" or "Taffy" and asked him on Mondays if he'd been down to Cardiff Arms Park at the weekend.'

'You're talking about Glyn Morgan.'

Her face lit up. 'You know him? How is he? I haven't seen him for years.'

'He's well, apart from hay fever. Did you know Gary Carr as well?'

She sobered. 'We're all very sorry about Gary. Do you know if the police have found out anything yet? What about Christine Gregory? Do you know her too?'

'I'm not sure. Glyn's wife is called Christine.'

She grinned delightedly. 'It's sure to be. Did she keep the baby then, if she got married?'

'Keep her? Why shouldn't she?'

The woman looked embarrassed. 'Sorry, wrong baby. This one was a boy. You obviously don't know anything about it. Forget it.'

Mitchell shook his head. 'I'm sorry, I can't do that.' He introduced himself and showed her his warrant card. 'I'm working on Gary Carr's murder. Can you spare a few minutes to talk now or shall I come back later?'

She looked at her watch. 'I'm due for a tea break in ten minutes. I'll just finish serving your young lady and then it should be time.'

Mitchell looked round guiltily. He had forgotten all about Virginia. However, she immediately proved she would make some ambitious young detective an excellent wife. 'I'll spend the next hour in C&A, Benny. Meet me outside at half-past four, prepared to buy me a particularly expensive tea.' She made a final selection of books, paid for them and left them behind for her swain to carry.

Mitchell found his all-day pub, backed by a little bricked courtyard. Miss Marriott proved a willing recipient of the pint he'd intended for Virginia. They sipped in silence for a minute, letting the perspiration evaporate.

'I don't know that I can help you,' his companion offered, apologetically. 'I haven't seen the other three for years.' She set her glass down on the hot metal of the table top and watched the dark liquid cook from the bottom, bubbles rising.

'We haven't got all the answers from working on his recent circumstances. It could be that the reason for his death lies somewhere in the past.'

'I don't want to get anyone into trouble.'

'Not even Carr's killer?'

She looked shocked. 'Well, all right. Ask what you like.'

Mitchell drank deeply whilst his beer was still cool. 'Did you know Gerald Morgan too?'

'Not as well. He was only a fourth-former when we were in the lower sixth. The four of us knocked about together in school and out. Gary was the wild one. If we ever got into trouble it was usually over something he'd suggested but there was no harm in him really. Christine was quite a swinger at school and when we were out together but she was very quiet and docile at home because she had strict parents. Glyn and Gary were both keen on her but in those days she was interested in doing well at her A levels and just having a good time with all the crowd. Then one night we went to a party. There was a lot of drinking and none of us were used to it. We couldn't remember much about it afterwards and the hangovers we had put us off repeating the experiment. A bit later on Christine found she was pregnant. It must have happened that night because she wasn't that sort of girl. She'd only have got herself into that sort of situation by someone taking advantage of her. Well, she said she'd never slept with anyone otherwise and I think she was telling the truth.'

'Where did you fit in in all this?'

'At the party?'

'No, in general.'

'Well, I got as drunk as the others that night but usually I was the quiet one. I talked Gary out of some of his riskiest plans and I listened to the others and talked over their problems with them. On the whole, I preferred books to people. I still do, but I was fond of them at the time.'

Mitchell tried not to let his face register his opinion of this peculiar view of life as he listened in silence.

'Christine's parents took her away from school. They didn't believe in abortion. Nor did we. But they said the baby would have to be adopted. Christine didn't have much choice. She wasn't qualified for a decent job. Her parents wouldn't help by looking after the infant during the day anyway and there weren't lots of nurseries and child minders around then. She and I talked about it for hours and Christine thought it would have a better chance with adoptive parents. She became as quiet as me after he'd been taken away. As soon as he was old enough to stop looking like a dried-up vegetable and to begin looking like a small human it was obvious he was Gary's but Mrs Gregory made Christine put "father unknown" on the birth certificate.

'Gary's family could see the likeness and were furious with him. They made him leave school too to avoid some of the gossip. He got a job in a garage and moved into a bed-sitter. I got a job in a library in Manchester at that point. When I came home for Christmas Gary had disappeared and never got in touch, whilst Christine's family had moved to another town. Glyn read music here in Leeds and we both made new friends. I moved back recently to look after my father but I never met up with any of them again.'

She pulled a face as she took a mouthful of warm beer. 'That's all. The shop's phone number is on your girlfriend's receipts if you want to know anything else.' Mitchell thanked her, replaced her warm beer with a cold one, warned her not to put it down on the table and set off to find C&A.

On Sunday morning, Browne opened his front door to a resolute looking Mitchell. 'I need to speak to Virginia, sir,' Mitchell announced. The relationship had obviously reached a crisis. Browne called his daughter down and then made himself scarce in the study whilst Hannah retired to the kitchen to make noisy preparations for lunch.

They emerged when they heard the front door slam and met in the hall. Browne shrugged. 'At least they went out together. Did all that clattering achieve anything?' She shook her head. 'Right, then. We're going out for lunch.' Browne drove up the valley to his favourite Tiller and Tipple where he was fairly sure he would not encounter his constable or his daughter.

He could have lunched anywhere and been in no danger. The minds of both young people were far removed from thoughts of food. They were sitting on the low wall that surrounded the police station car park, where they were pretty certain, for a couple of hours at least, not to encounter Browne. They faced the front entrance which was two-storeyed on this side. A succession of decorative scrolls under the slates surmounted a row of long narrow windows, black-framed against yellow sandstone, clean and neat but not aggressively modern. The upper storey jutted slightly, casting the double doors of the main entrance in shadow and making them seem a little off-putting to the innocent enquirer. The crane being used to complete the tower block behind looked like a complicated aerial on the roof.

Their view of the building had been softened, until they were close up to it, by courtesy of the Methodist church opposite, whose garden lay alongside. On a black metal pole by the porch three spherical lights of opaque white glass were mounted, very like those outside the excellent fish and chip shop a couple of streets away from Mitchell's home.

The sun glittered on the red crest of the West Yorkshire Police badge and the quartz chips in the car park flags. Behind them a black and yellow notice warned, 'Caution – emergency vehicles leaving yard', but the white vans were stationary, parked in neat rows.

Virginia was angry and Mitchell was enjoying it. Her eyes flashed, almost rivalling the effect of the sun glinting on her diamanté earrings. She was young enough to be forgiven for wearing them in the morning and with a sleeveless cotton dress, and attractive enough to get away with it. If Mitchell had had the discrimination and temerity to see and point out that they were breaking the rules of good taste, she would have replaced them with larger ones and he would have applauded her. The dark heavy lock of hair that fell over her forehead just like her father's made her hotter and crosser.

She dropped her gaze so that she could remain angry but was finding it increasingly difficult. She loved it when Benny was high-handed with her. Not that she had any intention of taking the meek little woman rôle but he was a fit antagonist. She could let fly at him, demolish his arguments, say exactly what she thought and felt without having a guilty conscience about hurting his feelings. She could make him angry with her, she could make him reconsider his point of view but she couldn't dint his self-esteem.

There was something very satisfying and comfortable about that. Not like that wimp David Draper whom she'd gone out with last year. He'd been talented, of course. At school they'd been sure he'd be famous one day. Dad had told her to hang on to the pencil sketch he'd done of her. That was no use though, when she had to watch her tongue all the time, knowing that he agonised over her every criticism and grumble. She didn't want that responsibility.

She risked another glance at Benny. The maddening smile was still there as he waited to be amused by her next outburst of temper. 'Let me get this straight. You want me to go to Oxford in October with a great dent made in my reading list. Then Dad will think you're a good influence on me and smile on our relationship and back your promotion. The fact that I have other ideas is irrelevant.' She stamped her foot in frustration as he shook his head, still smiling.

'Not seeing each other so often will be a pity and I freely admit that it's important to me that there should be no recriminations from your father but I've better reasons than that for holding out for a graduate wife.'

Now she was startled, too much so to speak. He, too, was comparing this relationship with the others in his past. What a change from Melanie. What a mercy there'd been no repercussions from that little fling. With Virginia there was no posing, no provocative dressing, though no false modesty either. She had a very healthy self-respect that made it unnecessary for her to have his approval unless she was trying to please him. She was still looking away but listening hard.

'One of us ought to have some academic qualifications, just in case it's still any use. It'll be a spur to me. I'll have to become at least a commander to rival it. If you don't get a degree you'll be denying me my motivation. And, although I could live with the annoyance of your father blaming me, I couldn't live with the fear that you might hold it against me, or at least have regrets about it. If you go and then feel you've done the wrong thing you won't have lost anything. You'll still be young enough to try something else. And, damn it all, Ginny, when you've finished all this posing you know that underneath you really want to go.'

Now she turned and looked hard at him and they remained still, equally unembarrassed by her scrutiny. She saw middle height and a stocky build, thick brown hair with a police regulation cut even though it was no longer required of him, muscular arms and blunt features, both with a healthy tan, and brown eyes, kind and uncompromising at the same time. 'Have you just proposed to me?'

He grinned. 'No, but I've made it quite clear that when the time's right I intend to.'

179

She wrinkled her nose. 'That's messing about, Benny. If you tell me you're going to then you more or less have done.'

After a long pause he asked, quite casually, 'And what do you more or less think about it?'

She walked away from him and gazed without seeing it at her father's favourite view of the busy little town centre below. After a couple of minutes she came back to him. 'I won't marry you for several years but I'll go to Oxford wearing your ring.'

He let out a long breath. 'So that's the bargain?'

'No. You were serious about the proposal. That's what I've decided.'

He swung her round and they set off walking hand in hand. She added in a lighter tone, 'Please God Dad's in a good mood.'

Browne had enjoyed an excellent three-course lunch and his equal share of an even more excellent bottle of Châteauneuf du Pape. A pleasant walk along the canal bank had helped to digest both and his cellphone had remained silent. The walk had also deepened his suntan and, although he was not deliberately cultivating it, it confirmed his impression, when he caught sight of his newly showered reflection, that really he was wearing quite well. When Hannah reminded him how wise he had been in always allowing his children, once they had reached years of discretion of course, to make their own decisions, he was able to congratulate the young couple. He even used quite a friendly tone when he reminded Mitchell that the inquest on Gary Carr began at nine the next morning.

Chapter 20

The inquest brought no surprises and was adjourned pending further enquiries. Fenwick had appeared in white shirt, sober conservative suit and dark tie and Hunter had to agree with the doctor that he inspired more confidence when he dressed to please himself. To everyone's relief, the body was released for burial, the HO pathologist declaring that he had taken a welter of samples and it could tell him no more. Theresa Carr having provisionally anticipated this, the undertakers were able to book the funeral for Wednesday morning. In every other respect, Monday and Tuesday were negative days. Reports were studied ad nauseam. There was no news from Holland concerning Bill Mellor. A considerable amount of work was devoted to less serious crimes.

It was decided that Hunter should attend the funeral, representing both the police and the church choir. The hot weather had carried on relentlessly into Wednesday and Hunter was pleased with his lot. Through the stained glass the sun drew coloured patterns on the upper walls but the well of the church with its dark wood, fresh-looking white plaster and faded blue aisle carpet was dim and cool. The Mothers' Union banner, propped in the corner beside the Communion table, provided a splash of colour. The flowers were simple, just small white posies on the sills and the coffin.

'Good thing those showy jobs of Mrs Hunter's have been taken away. Mrs Garside knows what's right.' The tactless whisper from behind caused Annette to bite her lip. Hunter felt a fierce wave of anger. The festival arrangements had been still reasonably fresh and Annette had originally planned to leave them at least another week. She had spent more than two hours the previous evening taking them away and replacing them with decorations that were more fitting to the occasion and which she thought would please Theresa.

181

Glyn Morgan had plumped for 'proper organ music, inexpertly executed' rather than 'a competent repetition of hymn tunes' and was having rather the worst of a battle with a Bach prelude. Hunter looked round surreptitiously. Mrs Kelly had apparently not been well enough to attend. Zoe sat in the front pew with the immediate family and her parents sat behind. Behind them was Mr Watmough with someone who was probably a colleague. He saw, but failed to recognise, Jessica Marriott who had been informed of the arrangements by Mitchell. All the expected church members were there. He heard a sharp intake of breath from Christine Morgan who had also been gazing around. She hurriedly faced the front again. Hunter ventured another turn of his head and saw a youth come in and seat himself at the back. He bore a resemblance to Frank; some cousin no doubt. Then he looked at the lad again and recognised Charles Atkinson. What was he doing here?

There was no sermon and no reference to the manner of Carr's death. Hunter knew that several choir members had offered to take time off work to sing an anthem but Gary had not been musical and Theresa had chosen the shortest form of the simple spoken service. The twenty-third psalm, included because it was the only one Gary would have recognised, was spoken too. Perhaps as an act of atonement, Frank had offered to read the lesson. 'Do not let your hearts be troubled,' was delivered shakily. Anne-Marie, in a navy suit, sat and stood and knelt with the congregation but remained mute.

Hunter had been home to change before he reported to Browne's oven of an office. Browne had been very interested in Atkinson's presence in church and, maddeningly refusing to explain, had sent for Bellamy. 'I think Sergeant Hunter has been haunted,' he told him when he appeared, 'by that ghost of a motive you were looking for.' Bellamy looked first mystified, then excited, and finally, because Hunter rather than himself had made the discovery, disappointed.

Browne told both men to report their doings to each other and amused himself, as they talked, by watching light dawn on each. 'We'll all call on Mr Atkinson,' he told them. 'Our concerted weight should persuade him to reveal all.'

This time there was no meeting in progress at Priestley's house.

In fact there was no sign of Priestley at all. When Atkinson opened the door he had a bottle of walnut oil in one hand. He seemed less than surprised to see them. 'I'm making a salad dressing. Do you want Alan?' Browne shook his head. 'Well, can we talk in the kitchen? Alan's speaking at a women's meeting this afternoon so he'll need lunch on time.'

When Browne nodded he led the way through and began counting drops of oil into a jug. Now he had noticed it, Hunter found Atkinson's likeness to Frank so marked that in spite of longish hair and the beard he couldn't understand how he'd missed it the first time he'd interviewed him.

'We're interested,' Browne announced, 'in why you chose to attend Gary Carr's funeral this morning.' Atkinson put down the bottle of oil and began adding vinegar to the mixture in the jug. 'A budding journalist are you? Or thinking of going into the church?'

Atkinson put down the vinegar bottle, faced Browne and drew himself up to his full height. 'I think I have just as much right as anyone else to be present at my father's funeral.'

'And as much of a duty to help find his killer.'

Atkinson shrugged. 'If you think anything I can tell you would help. Carr was my father and Christine Morgan is my mother.'

Browne pulled up a chair and motioned to his colleagues to do the same. 'Better late than never, I suppose.' Bellamy took out a notebook. Atkinson looked hard at him, then continued to prepare the complicated salad.

Suddenly, words poured out of him. 'My adoptive parents brought me up in Derbyshire. My father died when I was twenty-one and it was only from the terms of the will that I found out that I had been adopted. It didn't upset me. I found it quite an interesting idea. It made me decide to confide in my mother that I was homosexual.'

'Why did it?' Browne was thankful to find he referred to the matter in a straightforward way. Egg yolk was being added carefully to the contents of the jug.

'Well, I like being honest but my mother's a bit conventional. I thought if she found the idea hard to accept she might blame herself. But if I was someone else's son it was different.'

'How did she take it?'

'She went mad. Threw me out. That didn't worry me much

183

either. I'd always got on better with my father and I'd begun to get itchy feet. It was two years since I'd lived at home except during the vacs and Dad had left me quite well off. I'd have liked to have made a grand gesture and refused the money but I've more common sense than that and I wouldn't be earning for another year. I decided to finish my degree course and then spend the summer after finals finding my real parents. I saw a social worker who got me a copy of my birth certificate and then I agreed to be counselled. That was a laugh. They advised me against going ahead. I drew my own conclusions. If it had been inconvenient to have me around at six weeks it was going to be even more so at twenty-two. Still, when the social services were reluctant to play ball, I had enough money to try other people.'

Driven to distraction, Browne broke in. 'For God's sake stop making that clatter!'

Atkinson put down the offending jug and fork and pulled up a chair for himself before continuing. 'I decided to use a private detective. I found one in the phone book though it was more difficult than you'd think from reading stories. I gave him the birth certificate and he tried all the school records in Leeds and advertised in the local press. The Gregorys might have seen it. I don't know. There was no reply anyway. The detective traced my mother by chance. Her much younger sister had a baby and although they'd moved away they put a notice in the *Yorkshire Post* to let their old friends know. That gave us something to go on.'

'But weren't you put off when the social workers told you your blood relations didn't want to hear from you?'

Atkinson waved his hands, trying to find the words to explain. 'The idea of me wasn't welcome, as a ghost from the past, but they hadn't rejected me as a real person. They might have quite liked me when they met me. I could just have called round and introduced myself but I wanted to observe them and let them get to know me without them knowing it was me. Do you mind if I smoke?'

Browne considered. 'I do but it isn't my house.' Atkinson had been well brought up by the mother who had rejected him and deferred to the wishes of his uninvited guest.

'Going to church seemed a good way to mix with them. I hinted to them that I didn't know anyone around here and they were more or less obliged to invite me for a meal.' Browne wondered what Garside would make of this reason for church attendance and decided he would accept it happily along with all the others. 'They chose a day when Zoe was out. I don't know whether they had a premonition of the shock I was going to give them or whether they wanted to keep their pure and sinless daughter away from a homosexual.'

Browne smiled. 'You obviously haven't got to know Zoe very well.'

'I thought Glyn was my father till that day. When the meal was over he took me off to a pub miles away and told me the real story. He tried to buy me off. He had a shock when he discovered that I could have bought him three times over. I told him that if both of my parents were embarrassed by my presence I wouldn't need paying to go away. I thought at first it was because of the sex thing but I soon realised it was because he worshipped my mother and he couldn't bear her reputation to suffer, especially in Zoe's eyes.'

'It sounds as though he doesn't know Zoe very well either. So you went to see Carr?'

'Yes, the same night.'

'And?'

'He was interested. He talked. He asked about my degree course and the life I'd lived. We both got a bit drunk, especially him and on remarkably little grog. He obviously wasn't much of a drinker. He began going round the pub, boasting about what I'd told him. Glyn Morgan came in then. I don't think it was by accident either. We managed to get my father outside before he threw up, then we took him home. I told him I'd move on pretty soon since my mother's family didn't want to know me. I was going to keep in touch with my father.'

The heat hit them as they came outside again. Browne grinned. 'I'm not sure Priestley is going to appreciate haute cuisine for rabbits. He strikes me as a pie and chips man,' he remarked as they climbed into the insufferably hot car.

Bellamy, settling himself at the wheel, turned. 'Is it the Morgans' next?'

Christine Morgan opened the door immediately they rang the bell. She had obviously been expecting them since her son had put in his unscheduled appearance that morning and Browne decided to help her by revealing everything they knew about her already. She listened quietly, her face an expressionless blank, nodding or shaking her head from time to time. When he had finished Browne gave her a moment to calm the turmoil of thoughts she had not expressed, then asked, 'What can you add to that story?'

She spoke as though from a long way away. 'When the baby grew so like Gary, the scandal blew up all over again. I called him Martin for the few weeks I had him. He kept that as his middle name. My mother refused to see the likeness. I couldn't support him and my mother wouldn't help. I thought he'd have a better life if I let him go. He did too. I'd wanted to go to university but I couldn't face going back to re-do A levels so I worked till Glyn got his degree and then we got married. Gary's parents did believe the baby was his. They made him leave school before his exams as a punishment. Can you imagine anything more stupid and vindictive? He was only seventeen and he never qualified for anything to suit his ability. He just went from job to job, never finding anything that absorbed or satisfied him.

'He never blamed me for it though or minded that I married Glyn. Soon afterwards Gary met Theresa. She was doing a degree at Leeds but she travelled every day from Cloughton. Her grant was smaller living at home and that suited Mrs Kelly because Theresa had less independence. She had never had such a good time even though, by his standards, Gary had sobered up a lot. We both had. She married him as soon as she had finished her studies but it went wrong quite early on. Gary planned to do a degree part time but in those days Theresa wasn't the self-reliant body she is now. She wasn't up to seeing Gary through five years' studying. Besides, she's a Catholic and the children were on the scene pretty quickly.'

Browne, who was not in a position to offer such an opinion, was glad when Hunter interrupted. 'If you get a suitable opportunity, it might be a good thing to try to explain some of his father's frustrations to Frank. It would help him to live with his father's memory more easily than he could with his actual person.'

She nodded and continued. 'Theresa was frightened of the responsibility and disillusioned when Gary the husband was different from Gary the carefree lover. She went back to sheltering under her mother's wing.'

'You've kept in close touch since your schooldays then?'

'Oh, no. Until this estate was built and by chance we bought neighbouring houses, we hadn't seen them for years. Theresa knows Gary had an illegitimate child when he was still at school but she doesn't know I did. Zoe knows nothing about any of it and Glyn's desperate that she shouldn't find out. When we discovered the Carrs were to be our neighbours I thought there might be some awkwardness between Glyn and Gary but it was Theresa that Glyn couldn't get on with. He thinks she's cold, ungenerous, rigid in her demands. He was sorry for Gary.

'Gary got drunk when he met up with Martin again – Charles, I mean. Glyn brought him here before he'd had a chance to reveal all. When he'd sobered up he still wanted to acknowledge our son and keep in touch. I wouldn't have minded and I'm sure Zoe would have taken it in her stride. But since the lad is as self-reliant and personable as he is, and not needing any material help from us, and since Glyn feels as he does, I decided to let him go. Glyn's always been jealous of my part in that short fling with Gary and since the two families had settled down well together I didn't want anything happening to upset matters.'

When they left she was still trying to shift the guilt for her son's rejection to her husband's shoulders and seemed to have no conception of the implications of what she'd said. Bellamy climbed into the driving seat once more, alight with triumph. 'The man himself now?'

'No,' said Browne. 'Later. I don't think she'll warn him off. The garage was your pigeon too, young Nigel. Get to a phone and see whether the Dutch have yielded up our friend Mellor, either at work or at home. Make him lead us to that box.' He glanced at Hunter but the sergeant was smiling, quite happy for hard-working DCs to be given their rewards so long as they weren't called Mitchell.

Chapter 21

Theresa Carr watched the three policemen leave number twenty-one and wondered whether to try to talk to Christine. Was it fair to burden her with it all? At least she was a grown woman and not involved in it. She could be used as a sounding board and perhaps she would offer the advice that Theresa was becoming desperate for. But what if she refused to keep it secret? But here there was only Frank she could talk to and there was more guilt and responsibility on his shoulders than she'd had any right to put there. It was either talk to Christine or go mad.

The hinges on number twenty-one's gate squeaked, bringing Christine to the door, glad to be distracted from the uncomfortable feeling that, at her husband's unreasonable request, she had given her son less than he deserved. Theresa's face drove all thoughts of herself from her mind. She drew her friend into the hall, placed her in an easy chair and poured a small brandy. 'I'll hear about it when you've drunk that. It'll loosen your tongue. This looks like a trouble that wants halving by sharing.'

Theresa was glad she'd come and obediently emptied the glass. She felt eighty per cent better but the improvement was less the effect of the brandy than from having come to a decision.

Christine settled in the chair opposite. 'Ready?'

Theresa nodded. Keeping her eyes on the fingers that twisted in her lap, she spoke in a monotone. 'My mother wants to come and live with me, just when I'm beginning to break free of her. I can't do anything to get back my early life but at least I've wrenched back my middle age. But she's eighty now and frail and vulnerable. Out of pity, ordinary human feeling, I can't refuse. I've got the space.'

Christine sighed. She picked up the bottle and offered to refill Theresa's glass but Theresa shook her head. Christine spoke briskly. 'She uses any weapon she's got to get her own way. You know that. Now it's her helplessness. Have some sense. What's true or false has little meaning to your mother. She's only concerned with whether a particular remark or action will get the response she's after, get the other person to behave in the way she wants. Yes, she is old and frail, but the warden's always on call and the three of you visit often.'

'I know, but I haven't been listening.' A tear trickled down the colourless cheek. Christine was aghast. Theresa never cried. 'I've just been watching her lips move and shutting out the whine and giving automatic answers. I blame myself for not realising to what a pitch she'd driven herself.'

Christine had heard all this before and not just once. She wondered what trouble had blown up now to make Theresa so much more upset than usual. Still, she was looking better. If listening for another half hour would help, Christine could spare the time.

Browne was keeping another appointment with his hateful paper-work and looked up with a smile when Mitchell appeared in his doorway. 'Sit down, Benny. Glad to be interrupted.'

Mitchell began diffidently. 'Sir, you remember me saying that I'd noticed a similarity between Mrs Kelly's symptoms and nicotine poisoning. Sergeant Hunter wasn't too impressed with the idea but I couldn't get it out of my head. Then I thought . . .'

Browne's telephone rang. 'Just a minute, Benny.' Browne listened and nodded. 'Mellor's downstairs,' he told Mitchell. 'By the time Bellamy rang the garage, they'd told him we wanted him and he was on his way. You can sit in if you're quiet.'

Mellor got straight to the point. He had a garage to put to rights after a week's absence. 'That wooden box? Mrs Kelly sent for it by phone. They get high-handed like that when they're older. My old mother thinks the rest of the world's there to wait on her. I wouldn't have put myself out too much but a wheelchair had to be delivered to one of them flats so the box went with it.'

'When?'

'Morning of Tuesday the thirty-first.'

Bellamy was desperate to get the bottle and have it printed but Dean was chosen. He walked off disgustedly after Mellor.

As though there'd be any prints on it now! Browne turned back to his first visitor. 'What was your idea, Benny?'

'Well, sir, another side of the first one and it backs up Mr Mellor's information. Nicotine is easily absorbed through skin contact. Mrs Kelly probably didn't realise that.'

'When she measured out her son-in-law's fatal dose? Hunter and I owe you an apology, Benny. You'll be mentioned in despatches.'

Christine had long since stopped listening but she was recalled by having her arm grabbed as Theresa reached the climax of her tale. 'She just decided what she wanted and by grumbling or some other unpleasantness forced other people, usually me, to provide it. But getting rid of Gary was more than even she could get someone else to do for her. She did it herself, although she got Frank and me to cope afterwards. And now she wants to be with me because she's frightened of letting slip what she's done. What can I do?'

Christine tried to keep her hands still and to speak calmly. 'You've already done it. You've told me and you did it to save yourself and your children. You didn't really expect me to connive in this. I'll ring the police now.'

She went out into the hall and Theresa heard her voice though not the words. Presently Christine came back and put her arm round Theresa's shoulders. 'It's all right. You didn't shop her. They'd already sent out a car to bring her in.'

St Oswald's had had the good manners and common sense not to turn up at the funeral service in droves. Fewer than two dozen people were seated in the two front pews and just Hunter and Browne further back. There was a general atmosphere of sorrow mixed with relief. The white posies that had graced the son-in-law's funeral were doing duty again, still fresh and pretty.

This time Frank had not felt equal to reading the lesson and he listened to the vicar's firm reiteration, 'Do not let your hearts be troubled.' It was easier said than done, he decided. On the whole he was thankful that the arrival of the squad car at Gran's door had precipitated another heart attack. Neither he nor Mum had wanted her to get over it. Things were best like this.

The policeman called Bellamy had been sorry for Gran. He'd heard him talking to one of the others. He thought Gran had really believed what she had read in Anne-Marie's diary and had just been trying to protect her granddaughter. Frank had been there and knew the truth. He heard again the hissing voice, excited and scared but full of hatred for the man who, in her opinion, had considered his responsibilities to her daughter of so little account. She had described her ruse to obtain the pesticide with a kind of crazed triumph. Her own sufferings from contact with it had not diminished the self-congratulation with which she related the doctoring of his father's coffee and his quick end. Frank was thankful at least for that.

He felt as though it were someone else who had taken charge, who had decided that, although his grandmother was probably mad, she was not a danger to anyone else. He couldn't believe that he had calmly soothed his mother, treated her shock with sweet tea, got her to phone for the doctor, driven off to collect a wheelchair bag and stowed it, its dreadful contents carefully sealed, in the Mini's boot. He didn't want to think about what he and Mum had done on Saturday night.

Mum might marry Gerald in a few years' time. He wouldn't have pleased Gran either. He had too many ideas of his own. He'd look after Mum though, and, if not, he'd be able to do it himself before too long. She'd manage to carry on for the next five years like she had for the last five. And when he'd become a vet he'd really be able to contribute something substantial.

Anne-Marie didn't seem to have learned anything. She'd been scribbling in that diary again this morning. He shook his head to clear it and gave his attention to the service again. It had almost finished. 'Unto Him that is able to keep us from falling, and to present us faultless before the presence of His glory with exceeding joy . . .' Frank liked that idea. 'Amen,' said the congregation and Frank filed out with them into the still dazzling sunshine.

The mourners clustered in the porch so that Frank couldn't get through. Being too polite to push, he leaned against the baking stonework and listened idly to what the vicar was saying to Inspector Browne. 'You probably think our minds should be on higher things and, momentarily, at intervals during the service, they are – at different times for each person taking part. And that's an achievement. Divine worship is an exhausting and frightening business. We're only too glad to be distracted from it by hymns and prayers.' They were both smiling.

Frank turned away. He didn't know what the vicar was talking about and Zoe was waiting for him at the gate.